SOCIAL EMOTIONAL LEARNING WORKBOOK FOR ELEMENTARY

Navigating Emotions With Grade Level Activities

Richard Bass

2 Free Bonuses

Receive a *FREE* Planner for Kids and a copy of the
Positive Discipline Playbook by scanning below!

Contents

Chapter 2: First Grade–Building Empathy

SOCIAL EMOTIONAL
LEARNING WORKBOOK
FOR ELEMENTARY

Navigating Emotions With Grade Level Activities

Introduction

Understanding Social-Emotional Learning

It takes courage to grow up and become who you really are. There are better starters than me but I'm a strong finisher.

-Usain Bolt

Welcome to the world of social-emotional learning (SEL), where students are taught how to develop healthy identities, attitudes, and relationships through social and emotional skills training. Through this process, students are prepared for the sometimes unexpected challenges that occur inside and outside of the classroom, from how to regulate explosive emotions to learning how to build and nurture peer relationships.

The focus of this workbook is on teaching elementary-aged students critical SEL skills that can empower them to manage stress, show empathy toward others, build resilience, form strong bonds with peers, and so much more. Practicing these skills can also assist with the management of challenging behaviors in the classroom that interfere with students' ability to follow instructions, solve problems, engage in classroom discussions, and build meaningful relationships with others.

Research shows that a curriculum that promotes SEL can boost academic performance, improve mental wellness, and foster healthy peer relationships (CASEL, n.d.). These positive outcomes are partly due to the five core social and emotional competencies that are taught and reinforced in the classroom, which include:

1. **Self-awareness:** The recognition of how your thoughts and emotions impact your attitudes and behaviors
2. **Self-management:** The ability to accept responsibility for your actions and manage how you respond to social situations
3. **Social awareness:** The recognition of social cues and understanding of how others respond to your behaviors and communication
4. **Responsible decision-making:** Acknowledging that you have a choice in how you respond to situations and practicing good decision-making by weighing the benefits and consequences of your actions
5. **Relationship skills:** The ability to form and maintain healthy relationships with others and the ability to communicate effectively in order to show empathy and avoid conflict and misunderstandings

For students to master these five competencies and become self-aware and emotionally intelligent individuals both inside and outside of the classroom, they need to spend a lot of time practicing them. This workbook has made your planning a lot easier by offering 180 well-researched interactive activities to present to students at different elementary grade levels.

The Structure of the Workbook

What is the formula for a fun and educational workbook? A small amount of theory to provide context, and a massive amount of practical exercises to introduce and develop skills. This user-friendly workbook has been designed with teachers, students, and even parents in mind.

Teachers who recognize the crucial role of social-emotional learning in academic success and classroom discipline will be presented with over 100 different SEL activities that can be incorporated into classroom lessons and after-school programs. Each elementary grade level, from kindergarten to fifth grade, has been assigned 30 fun activities to complete over 30 school weeks. Teachers are more than welcome to borrow activities from grades below or above whenever they see fit.

The key piece to the puzzle is the students who will be guided through this transformative SEL journey. They will be captivated by the entertaining activities that seek to help them understand their emotions better and navigate social situations-both in and out of the classroom-with confidence.

Parents who are inspired by the social and emotional growth of their children can find ways to incorporate some of these activities at home in order to create a home-based learning environment. Doing this will strengthen their children's communication and relationship skills with family members and the broader community.

What unites teachers, students, and parents is the shared desire to build and master social and emotional skills that lead to holistic development, equipping students to succeed personally, socially, and academically. With this shared goal, students can confidently partake in the adventures and educational opportunities that await in this workbook.

The groundwork has been laid. Your mission is to approach this workbook with an open mind and a willingness to engage in self-reflection and growth, and encourage your students to do the same!

Chapter - 1

Kindergarten-Exploring Emotions

Life is not about waiting for the storms to pass... it's about learning how to dance in the rain.
- **Vivian Greene**

Introduction to Emotions

Emotions are like surprise visitors in our bodies. They can make us feel happy, sad, and sometimes, even a little confused. However, regardless of what form they come in, we need to accept all of our emotions, because they are helpful to us. Whether big or small, emotions can help us in the following ways:

- *Emotions can help us stay motivated when completing tasks.*
- *Emotions can help us find solutions to problems we are facing.*
- *Emotions can alert us when we are feeling uncomfortable in our bodies.*
- *Emotions can help us express to others what we need.*
- *Emotions can help us make decisions about our actions.*
- *Emotions can help us understand our friends and family better.*

- *Emotions can help us avoid getting into trouble at school and at home.*

Sometimes, when emotions surface in our bodies, it isn't clear what they are. We scratch our heads, wondering, "Am I feeling angry or am I feeling sad?" So, to avoid confusion around our emotions, we need to learn more about them and understand how they come about and how to recognize them.

The following interactive activities can help us learn more about emotions and how to recognize them.

30 Weeks of Fun: Emotion Recognition Activities for Kindergarten Students.

Learning about emotions gives you more control over them. You can easily identify what you are feeling and decide on the best way to cope with it. Here are 30 interactive activities that will boost your confidence in identifying and managing your emotions.

Activity 1: Miming Magic

Did you know that you can tell how someone feels just by looking at their face? It's true! In our fun game called Miming Magic, one student gets to be the actor, and everyone else is the audience. The actor thinks of a feeling, like being happy or sad, and shows it with their face without saying any words. If the actor needs help, they can pick a feeling from a hat. Then, the audience raises their hands and tries to guess the feeling. The first person to guess right gets to be the actor next! It's like a magical guessing game with expressions.

Here are some ideas for the type of emotions you can act out:

- surprised
- sad
- embarrassed
- mad
- happy
- bored
- jealous
- tired
- proud
- scared
- lonely

Activity 2: Feelings Matchup!

Every emotion has its own special name. Learning these names can help you understand how you are feeling and talk about it better. It's hard to remember all the names at once, but you can start with the ones you hear most often and learn more as you go.

Now, here's a fun game to test how many feelings you know! Look at the faces below and match each one with the feeling word it represents. Use a ruler to draw lines connecting the faces to the words. Try your best, and when you're finished, show your teacher to find out how you did. Ready, set, go!

- Shy

- Interested

- Guilty

- Confident

- Proud

- Irritated

- Nervous

- Hurt

- Angry

Activity 3: Mood Masterpiece

Did you know that you can experience different emotions throughout the day? We call the changes in our emotions our "moods." For instance, your mood in the morning when you prepare for school may not be the same as your mood when you get to play with your friends.

Moods change whenever a new emotion surfaces. So, what is your mood right now? Close your eyes and put one hand to your chest, then ask yourself: "How am I feeling?" Think of a word that best describes your mood and draw a picture of yourself feeling that emotion. Continue to the end of the chapter for extra space in drawing your masterpiece or use the space below.

Activity 4: Emotion Piles

There are six basic emotions that form the building blocks for all the other emotions. These include **happiness, sadness, disgust, fear, anger, and surprise.** For example, happiness forms the building block for emotions like joy, peace, and confidence. Sadness forms the building block for emotions like loneliness, guilt, and hurt. Emotion Piles is an activity that seeks to help you recognize the building blocks of your emotions.

Go through each emotion illustrated on the table of words below and write them down in the correct "pile" or column underneath. In the end, there should be three emotions underneath each building block. Cross out emotions with an erasable pencil after you have placed them in piles so that you don't repeat them elsewhere. When you are done, show your teacher and get feedback.

Scared	Amazed	Furious
Awful	Panicky	Joyful
Grateful	Nervous	Disapproval
Mad	Unhappy	Irritated
Tearful	Shocked	Disappointment
Peaceful	Miserable	Startled

Happy	Sad	Disgust	Fear	Anger	Surprise

Activity 5: Going on an Emo-Venture!

Adventures are fun because you can explore your surroundings and discover new and interesting objects. An emo-venture is an adventure with a twist! Your teacher plays different songs on the music player, and you get to walk around the classroom and act out the emotions that are reflected in the songs.

Listen carefully to the words of the songs to understand what emotions are being displayed. Use your facial expressions and various parts of your body to bring the emotions to life. Whenever the music stops, stand still and wait for the next song to start playing, then start walking again while making different movements. Be bold and unleash your imagination to bring joy and laughter to the classroom.

Here is an age-appropriate playlist recommendation for teachers:

- Cry a Rainbow by Pierce Freelon and Nnenna Freelon
- The Happy Song by Imogen Heap
- I'm Mad by Matt Heaton
- I'm Scared by StoryBots
- Small Specks by Mil's Trills
- I Need a Break by Stephanie Leavell

Activity 6: The Tale of the Mysterious Emotions

Can you guess what time it is? It's story time!

Sit around your teacher and listen carefully as they read the book for today. After the book has been read, have a group discussion about the various emotions that were reflected by the different book characters. **Explore questions like:**
- *Who were the characters that appeared in the book?*
- *What emotions did they feel at the start and end of the book?*

- *Can you describe an emotion that a character felt using only facial expressions?*
- *Can you list the clues that helped you figure out what a character was feeling?*
- *Did the characters make good or bad choices based on what they were feeling?*

Activity 7: Sing-Along-With-Me

To recognize emotions, you need to be able to spell them out and write them down. This next fun game is a sing-along that you can play with your teacher. It encourages you to learn the names of emotions so that you can remember them.

To make this game enjoyable, clear your throat and unleash your best singing voice. Spend some minutes learning the rhyme or song lyrics with your teacher, then give it your best shot.

Note for the teacher: There are plenty of sing-along rhymes that you can modify to speak on emotions. Below is a modification of the nursery rhyme "B-I-N-G-O" using another five-letter emotion, "H-A-P-P-Y." Other five-letter emotions that you can alternate with are tired, angry, and proud.

Script:
There was a fellow in my school who felt happy all the time.

H-A-P-P-Y

H-A-P-P-Y

H-A-P-P-Y

They were happy all the time.

Activity 8: Mood Collage

Take a deep breath and check in with yourself. What is your current mood? What emotions do you notice?

For this next creative activity, you will make a collage of real people's faces. Find as many different facial expressions as you can find in the magazines provided for you. Take a pair of scissors and neatly cut out the pictures of the faces (if you need help, ask your teacher to assist you), and glue them onto the blank page at the end of the chapter. Make sure that the pictures overlap to avoid empty spaces.

When the entire class has completed their collages, take turns standing up by your desk and presenting the different emotions you have been able to find.

Activity 9: The Sock Puppet Show

Let's pretend that our feelings are like little people!

In The Sock Puppet Show, you get to act out your feelings with sock puppets! Find a partner and pick two feelings from a hat. Then, spend 10 minutes planning a short puppet show with your partner. You will need to make up a story that shows both feelings. Your teacher will set up a stage at the front of the class, and you will perform there.

Put a sock on one of your hands, and decorate it to look like a person with eyes, lips, and hair if you like. When it's showtime, kneel down so only your hands are visible, and have fun acting out your puppet show for your classmates!

Activity 10: Emo-Mimic Madness

Facial expressions make it easier for you to communicate what you are feeling when you can't find the right words. On the other hand, learning how to read and mimic other people's facial expressions helps you understand what they might be feeling.

Emo-Mimic Madness is a game best played in pairs. Stand or sit at a table facing your partner and take turns mimicking each other's facial expressions. For example, you might start by expressing sadness and their job is to mirror back the sadness in the same style. Afterward, it's their turn to express a different emotion on their face, which you must mirror back to them.

Activity 11: Emotion Weather Chart

Have you looked at the weather forecast for your moods today? Is there a high chance of brightly sunny emotions or gloomy emotions? On a large sheet of paper, create your own emotion weather chart that you can fill out each day. The purpose of the chart is to help you identify the emotions you are feeling each day based on different weather conditions. Here are common weather conditions and the types of emotions they can represent:

- Sunny = Happy or excited
- Partly cloudy = Worried or bored
- Rainy = Sad or lonely
- Stormy = Angry or disappointed

Before or after class, check in with yourself and assess how you are feeling. Place a check mark under the relevant weather conditions, and share your discovery with your teacher. When sharing your feelings with others, you can refer to the weather conditions. For example, you could say, "I am feeling sunny today because it's my birthday!" or "I am feeling stormy today because my friend won't share their toys with me!"

Here is an example of what your emotion weather chart could look like. Include pictures on your chart to represent the different weather conditions.

	Sunny	Partly cloudy	Rainy	Stormy
Monday				
Tuesday				
Wednesday				
Thursday				
Friday				
Saturday				
Sunday				

Activity 12: Taking the Opposite Action

Big emotions like anger, sadness, and loneliness can sometimes cause you to make wrong choices like yelling, hitting others, spitting, or throwing your toys. These choices end up hurting other people and make the situation worse.

Whenever big emotions rise to the surface, take some time to cool down and think about the opposite action that you can take. For example, the opposite action for yelling would be to speak with a gentle voice. Taking the opposite action can help you calm your emotions and respond positively to situations.

The following table presents common behaviors that you might practice whenever you feel big emotions like anger and sadness. Your task is to write down what you believe is the opposite action that you can take to improve the situation.

When I feel like YELLING, I can take the opposite action and...

When I feel like KICKING SOMEONE, I can take the opposite action and...

When I feel like SPITTING, I can take the opposite action and...

When I feel like PUSHING SOMEONE, I can take the opposite action and...

When I feel like THROWING OBJECTS, I can take the opposite action and...

Activity 13: The Emotion Guessing Jar

There's a fun game called the Emotion Guessing Jar that everyone in class can play! The goal is to pick something from a jar or big box and say how it makes you feel and why. Like, if you pick a soft feather, it might remind you of feeling calm and peaceful. But if you pick a fidget spinner, it could make you think of being jittery or excited.

And guess what? You can even make a cool show-and-tell presentation about the object you pick! If you need help matching the object with the right feeling, just ask your teacher for hints or ideas. Have fun guessing and sharing feelings with your classmates!

Activity 14: Storytelling With Emotion Stones

Painting faces on stones is like giving them their own feelings and stories! To do this fun activity, bring a small stone to school. Think about a feeling you want to paint on it, like being happy, sad, or silly. Use lots of colors to show how you feel.

After you're done painting, let your stone dry for a while. When all the stones are dry, we'll get into groups and make stories with them. Each group will share their story about the feelings on their stones with the class.

Activity 15: Musical Chairs With an Emotional Twist

Do you remember how to play musical chairs, the game where chairs are placed in a row (minus one) and music is played while you walk around the chairs? The challenge is to quickly find a chair and sit down when the music suddenly stops.

In this game, we provide an emotional twist, which is to ask the last student standing (the student without a chair) a question about their emotions. Students get to choose their own questions from the pile of flash cards below. After they have answered their questions, they can return to the group for the next round of musical chairs. The best part about this version of musical chairs is that nobody gets out of the game, so everybody can continue to have fun until the questions run out.

Here is a list of flash cards that you can use for the game. Feel free to cut them out so that you can spread them out on a table.

How are you feeling right now?

What makes you feel nervous?

Name one thing you are grateful for.

Name one thing that makes you feel proud of yourself.

What's the funniest thing that has happened today?

What puts you in a good mood when you are upset?

What is something kind that someone has done for you?

Tell a story about a time you felt happy.

What makes you feel angry?

How do you feel when someone says "I'm sorry" to you?

Activity 16: The ABCs of Emotions

You may be familiar with the letters of the alphabet, starting from A to Z. However, do you know the ABCs of emotions? To expand your emotion vocabulary and expose yourself to new words and sounds, you can learn and practice the names of different emotions that start with each letter of the alphabet.

Are you up for the challenge? Below are 26 flash cards with pictures, letters, and the names of different emotions. Challenge yourself to learn one emotion each day, until you can recite the whole alphabet. Your teacher can also set up a quiz to test how many emotions you can remember and spell out correctly.

15

The ABCs of Emotions

Angry
A

Bored
B

Confident
C

Delighted
D

Embarrassed
E

Frustrated
F

Gloomy
G

Happy
H

Irritated
I

Jealous
J

Kind
K

Lonely
L

Mad
M

Nervous
N

Overwhelmed
O

Proud
P

Quiet
Q

Relaxed
R

Sad
S

Tired
T

Unhappy
U

Valued
V

Worried
W

eXicted
X

Yearning
Y

Zealous
Z

Activity 17: How Would You Feel?

Do you ever wonder how you would feel if you were placed in certain situations? Imagining your emotional response to scenarios is a great way to address worries and feel prepared for whatever may come your way.

This game encourages you to use your imagination and picture yourself facing different situations. Take a moment to think about how you would feel if those situations happened. Use the emotion words that you have learned so far to provide meaningful responses.

Read the scenarios below and write down how you would feel if they occurred.

How would you feel if your parents bought you a new pet?	**How would you feel if you got a sticker for doing your best on an assignment?**	**How would you feel if your teacher raised their voice at you?**
How would you feel if your classmate refused to share their toys	**How would you feel if you got a sticker for doing your best on an assignment?**	
How would you feel if you didn't have anybody to play with?	**How would you feel if you lost your favorite toy or book?**	

Activity 18: The Emotion Clock

It's always a good time to talk about feelings! The Emotion Clock is a fun and creative activity that can help you feel confident to explore and share your emotions at school and at home.

For this activity, you will need a range of art supplies to create your custom cardboard clock, such as:

- *glue and scissors*
- *a paper plate to make your clock face*
- *colorful markers and crayons to decorate your clock*
- *other decorative supplies like paint and glitter*
- *two sticks or cardboard cutouts to make the clock hands*
- *a split pin to fasten the clock hands and make them movable*

Start by creating different facial expressions on the paper plate where you would normally see numbers. Ask your teacher to help you mark where each face should be on the clock. In total, you should end up with 12 different faces. Use various colorful pens and markers to make unique faces so that they each look distinct from the others.

After designing the faces, pick up the two sticks or cardboard hands and place them in the center of the paper plate with the two ends touching. Pin the ends together with a split pin. Make sure the pin goes through both ends and comes out on the other side of the plate. Separate the pin to secure it on the plate.

Well done! You have created your emotion clock. Now, it's time to play the game. Your teacher will go around the classroom and give students a turn to spin their clocks. When the two hands stop, students need to identify the emotions they are pointing at and describe an event or situation that made them feel that emotion. With your teacher's permission, you can take your emotion clock home and play the game with your family members as well.

Activity 19: Emotion Scavenger Hunt

Today, let's take the lesson outside and play a game of Emotion Scavenger Hunt. Your mission is to find as many different multicolored balls as you can in the playground. Each ball color represents an emotion. Here is an overview of what the colors mean:

- Red = **ANGRY**
- Blue = **SAD**
- Yellow = **HAPPY**
- Green = **CALM**
- Orange = **EXCITED**
- Purple = **CURIOUS**
- Pink = **LOVING**

Your teacher will give you time to collect colorful balls. When the time is up, return to the group and count how many balls you have collected and share with the rest of the class which emotions you were able to find.

Activity 20: Face Matchup Bingo

Here is another emotion recognition game that you can play as a class. For this game, you will need a black marker and a laminated bingo card that consists of 9 squares with different facial expressions inside of them.

The game starts with your teacher reading out an emotion. If you can find the matching facial expression on your bingo card, place a big check mark over the square. If you can't, wait for the next round to hear another emotion being called. Your teacher will continue reading out the names of emotions until a student gets three check marks in a row (e.g., vertically, horizontally, or diagonally). When this happens, the student should yell "BINGO!" They win that round, and the game starts all over again.

Activity 21: Peer Check-Ins

When did you last check up on your classmates to find out how they were feeling? Peer Check-Ins is a friendly game that involves having one-on-one conversations with your classmates in rotation. Your teacher will arrange desks in a straight line to create an interview setup. You can sit on any side of the desk that you like, facing anybody that you choose.

The timer will start, and you will have 2-3 minutes to check in with your classmates and find out how they are doing, and vice versa. Three simple questions to ask each other are as follows:

1. *How do you feel today?*
2. *What makes you happy?*
3. *What makes you sad?*

When the time is up, one side of the table needs to get up and move to the seat on their left, then the game starts again. Now you are facing somebody new who you can check in with. Continue to play the game until you have spoken to every classmate on the other side of the table.

Activity 22: Classroom Feelings Book

Writing down your emotions, whether it is happiness or sadness, can help you feel better. Work together with your teacher to create a classroom feelings book where you and other students can share your emotions whenever they have free time during the day. If you don't have the words to describe what you are feeling, feel free to draw a picture instead.

The classroom feelings book belongs to everybody in the class, so make sure that your classmates have an equal opportunity to use the book. At the end of the term, you can read through the different notes left by classmates and talk about the drawings.

Activity 23: Sensory Bottles

Did you know that you can use adjectives to describe your emotions? Adjectives are words that give you more information about how something looks or feels. For example, describing a ball as being **round** tells you more about its shape. Describing a dress as being **purple** tells you more about its color. There are also adjectives that you can use to describe how your emotions make you feel. Consider the following list:

- angry = hot
- sad = heavy
- happy = light
- excited = bouncy
- proud = warm
- lonely = empty
- scared = shaky
- frustrated = stuck
- relaxed = cool
- peaceful = quiet

Sensory Bottles is a creative activity that requires an empty bottle, art supplies, small objects that can fit inside a bottle, and some water. Your teacher will assign you an emotion to work with. Your job is to fill your bottle with small items that describe the emotion. For example, if you were given "Happy" as an emotion, you would need to look for items that are light, bright, vibrant, and beautiful. These could include items like a feather, glitter, and colorful beads.

Label your bottle with the emotion and place it on your desk. Walk around the other desks and see what your classmates have created. Give the bottles a good shake and observe how the materials move when you feel that emotion.

Activity 24: Making Faces With Playdough

Take a ball of playdough and challenge yourself to make faces displaying different emotions. Look at what your peers have created and try to guess what emotions are being displayed. If you have enough playdough, create a story using the faces you have created. Share the story with your classmates and listen to the tales that they have come up with.

Activity 25: Hello, and How Are You?

Start each morning with the emotions song. Line up outside of the classroom before school begins and wait to be greeted by your teacher, who will sing the song with you. When they say, "Hello, hello, hello, and how are you?" you must respond with the emotion you are feeling, like, "I'm joyful, joyful, joyful, and I hope that you are too." After you have greeted your teacher with the song, you may step inside the classroom.

Make facial expressions and change your voice according to the emotion you are feeling. For example, if you are feeling sad, sing the song in a slow and dreary voice with droopy eyes and a frown.

22

Activity 26: Ring Around the Emotions

Do you remember the game "Ring around the Rosie?" There is another version of the game that involves feelings. Go outside and stand in a circle with your classmates. Hold hands and begin to skip in a motion. Sing the song, "Ring around the rosie. A pocket full of posies. Ashes! Ashes! We all fall down!"

In the next round, change the action at the end to something that matches the emotion announced by your teacher. For example, if the emotion is anger, the action could change to "We all took a deep breath." If the emotion is sadness, the actions could be "We all hugged a friend."

Activity 27: Coloring Pages

It's time to take a break from working and spend time coloring pictures that display emotions. Flip over to the end of the chapter and color in the pictures given. Try to figure out why the characters in the picture feel the way they do. Use a range of colors to bring the emotion to life.

Activity 28: End of the Day Check-In

Before leaving the classroom at the end of the day, spend a few minutes reflecting on the emotions you felt during the day. Your teacher will go around the class asking each student how they felt. They will also ask you to complete the following sentence using your own words:

Today, I felt _____ when _____.

For example, you might say:
- *Today, I felt excited when we got to create Emotion Clocks.*
- *Today, I felt scared when I fell off the swing.*
- *Today, I felt proud when my teacher told me I did a good job.*

If you are embarrassed to share your emotions with the whole class, you can stay back and express them to your teacher.

Activity 29: Sing the Happy Song

Here is another sing-along that will get you up from your seat. Sing the song, "If You're Happy and You Know It," but for each round, change the emotion and the actions that go with it. For example, you might sing:

- *If you're happy and you know it, clap your hands.*
- *If you're sad and you know it, give a sigh.*
- *If you're mad and you know it, cross your arms.*
- *If you're tired and you know it, go to sleep.*

Can you think of any more ideas of emotions and actions that you can sing to? Present them to your teacher and give them a go!

Activity 30: What Do We Do?

When your classmates are feeling emotional, there is always something you can do to show that you care. Get into a group and brainstorm different ways that you can respond to your classmates when they are showing different emotions. Think about what you would do in various scenarios and bounce ideas off of each other. Assign one group member the role of the scribe who will write down the answers on the following worksheet. Share your responses with the rest of the class and have an open discussion.

If my classmate looked excited, I would...

_____

_____

If my classmate looked scared, I would...

_____

_____

If my classmate looked lonely, I would...

_____

_____

If my classmate looked confused, I would...

_____

_____

If my classmate looked furious, I would...

_____

_____

If my classmate looked bored, I would...

_____

_____

The ability to identify and correctly label your emotions allows you to better understand yourself and make good choices about how to respond to different situations. Continue to explore your emotions and learn new ways to describe how you are feeling.

Use the space below to draw a portrait of yourself based on the instructions given in Activity 3.

Use the space below to color in the picture represented below based on the instructions given in Activity 27.

Use the space below to color in the picture represented
below based on the instructions given in Activity 27.

Use the space below to color in the picture represented below based on the instructions given in Activity 27.

Chapter - 2

First Grade-Building Empathy

I am the master of my fate; I am the captain of my soul.

- William Ernest Henley

Introduction to Empathy

Empathy is like taking a walk in someone else's shoes to understand how they feel and what they think. It means putting our own feelings aside and trying to see things from their perspective.

Being empathetic is important because it shows us that everyone sees the world differently. When we listen to others and try to understand their experiences, we learn new things that can help us grow and become kinder people.

There are many different ways in which we can practice empathy in the classroom, such as:

- *showing respect for classmates who come from different cultures and backgrounds.*
- *noticing when some classmates are upset and going over to them to ask if they are okay.*

- *making sure that all classmates are included when playing games so that nobody feels left out.*
- *giving classmates an equal opportunity to speak when working on group projects.*
- *showing curiosity and asking questions to understand classmates who have different opinions and beliefs.*
- *being mindful of how our actions impact the people around us, like our teachers and classmates.*

Empathy is like a bridge connecting who we are with who other people are. When we put aside the urge to always be right and truly listen to what others have to say, we open ourselves to understanding their experiences better. Even when we don't agree with someone or understand their actions, we can still respect their thoughts and feelings.

Thankfully, there are 30 interactive activities offered below that can assist us in building and enhancing empathy in the classroom and beyond.

30 Weeks of Fun: Empathy-Building Activities for First-Grade Students

Do you wish that you could understand how other people are thinking and feeling so that you could say the right words and take the right actions? Perhaps what you need is more practice in building empathy and looking at the world from other people's viewpoints. Get ready to strengthen your empathy skills with the following interactive activities!

Activity 1: Understanding Through Acting

How you respond to someone's feelings can make things better. Understanding Through Acting is a fun game played in pairs. One person acts out an emotion, like being happy or sad. The other person shows empathy by choosing the best way to respond in a manner that makes their partner feel understood and respected. After that, switch roles and try a new emotion. This helps you learn what it feels like to be both the person showing feelings and the one responding to them.

Activity 2: Walking In Their Shoes

Thinking about how someone else feels means imagining what you would do if you were in their situation. In this game, we will use flash cards to talk about different problems that might happen with your classmates.

In smaller groups, you'll pick a few flash cards and talk about how you would handle the situations if you were the other person. Write down your ideas and share them with the rest of the class.

Feel free to cut out these flash cards to distribute them among the class.

Tanya left her homework at home for the third time in a row. She feels nervous about telling her teacher. What would you do if you were Tanya?

_____
_____
_____
_____
_____
_____

A new student, Daniel, has joined the class and feels shy because he doesn't know anybody. What would you do if you were Daniel?

_____
_____
_____
_____
_____
_____

During a group project, one of the group members, Jordan, feels frustrated because nobody is listening to what he has to say. What would you do if you were Jordan?

_____
_____
_____
_____
_____
_____

Angel approaches a group of classmates on the playground and asks to join them, but they say no and she feels left out. What would you do if you were Angel?

_____

_____

_____

_____

_____

Nivesh doesn't want to present his speech in front of the class because he is afraid of being laughed at. What would you do if you were Nivesh?

_____

_____

_____

_____

_____

_____

Activity 3: Empathy Listening Circle

Let's go outside and find a nice shady spot on the grass. Sit in a circle with your classmates. Your teacher will give one person a special talking stick (like a wooden spoon).

The person with the talking stick is the only individual allowed to talk. They can share how they're feeling or tell a story about something that happened to them. Everyone else should listen quietly. When the person is done talking, they will pass the talking stick to the person next to them on the left. The stick will go around the circle until everyone gets a chance to share something.

Activity 4: Movie Marathon

Watching movies is fun, but did you know it can also help us understand other people better? When we watch a movie, we become friends with the characters and see things from their point of view. We can understand why the heroes make good choices, and even why the villains make not-so-good choices.

This week, try to watch at least one of these movies. If you can't watch them in class, you can watch them at home as homework. Then, you can discuss them as a class when you come back to school.

Movie: Inside Out
Duration: 102 minutes
Age restriction: 6+ years
Discussion questions:

- *Why did Riley have a tough time telling her parents how she was feeling?*
- *How did Bing Bong feel the moment he helped Joy escape?*
- *What does the term "mixed emotions" mean? When would someone have mixed emotions?*

Movie: Beauty and the Beast
Duration: 90 minutes
Age restriction: 6+ years
Discussion questions:

- *Describe Belle's feelings when she decides to be the Beast's captive.*
- *Why was Gaston surprised when Belle decided she wouldn't marry him?*
- *How do the villagers see the Beast? Why do they want to get rid of him?*

Activity 5: Take a Trip to the Zoo

Let's go on a fun trip to the zoo! Spend the day watching the animals and seeing how they feel. Look at their faces, how they stand, and what they do. You might notice if they're happy, sleepy, or playful.

Animals can feel different things in different situations. For example, they might seem bored when they're alone, but when they see kids, they might get really excited! Bring a notebook to write down what you see, and we can talk about it when we get back to school.

Activity 6: Connecting the Dots With Photos

Let's have some fun with magazines! Bring some old magazines from home to school with you. Lay them out in front of you and look for pictures of people showing different feelings. They might be happy, sad, excited, or even surprised! Find five pictures you really like and cut them out carefully.

Once everyone has their five pictures, it's showtime! Stand up one by one and share your pictures with the class. Tell the class about the feeling in the picture and make up a story about why the person or people in the picture are feeling that way. Remember, it's all in your imagination, so let it run wild!

For example, for one photo, you might say "In this photo, a woman is holding a baby and looking happy. The reason she is happy is that her baby has just uttered their first word and she is very proud."

Activity 7: Social Detective Work

Did you know that besides using words, you can also tell others how you are feeling by how you move and look? It's like a secret language called body language! Body language is all the ways you show your feelings without talking, like making faces, using your hands, or even how you stand.

Understanding other people's body language sometimes requires you to be a detective because the clues aren't always easy to see. So, let's play a fun game! Find a partner, and one of you can use words while the other can only use their body to show how they feel. Here are some hints for the person using body language:

- **Smiling** is a sign of happiness, friendliness, and confidence.
- **Frowning** shows disapproval, sadness, or disappointment.
- **Raised eyebrows** suggest curiosity or the feeling of surprise.
- **The rolling of the eyes** is often a sign of irritation or impatience.
- **Crossed arms and legs** could signal discomfort or defensiveness.
- **Turning the body away** or looking away shows disinterest or discomfort.
- **Fidgeting or biting of the nails** can be signs of anxiety, boredom, or restlessness.
- **Nodding** shows approval or acknowledgment of what is being spoken.
- **Shaking the head** shows disagreement with what is being spoken.
- **Shrugging of the shoulders** is a sign of uncertainty or confusion.
- **Hugging** is a sign of friendliness and affection.
- **Raising the hand with the palm facing out** means stop and don't come closer.

After three minutes of role-playing, switch roles and come up with a new storyline. The nonverbal person should use different social cues to convey their messages.

Activity 8: Expressing My Gratitude

Gratitude is the practice of noticing and appreciating the good things that happen in your life. The things that you are grateful for can be big and small. For instance, you can feel grateful to have a friendly teacher or grateful for the delicious snacks you eat for lunch.

Take a moment to think about the things you are grateful for in your classroom. Use the flash cards below to write down your gratitude list, then discuss them with your classmates.

I feel grateful for

I feel grateful for

I feel grateful for

I feel grateful for

I feel grateful for

Activity 9: The Empathy Relay Race

Here's another activity that you can play outside. You will need two teams. Each team will run a race and pass a baton, but here's the twist: The baton has feelings written on it! When you pass it, your teammate has to show that feeling with empathy before they run. Like, if it says 'sadness,' they can give a comforting hug. If it says 'excitement,' they can do a happy dance! Try to be creative and not do the same thing twice. The team that finishes first wins!

Activity 10: Seeing the Other Side

Everybody has an opinion about what they like or dislike or how they would handle situations. Your opinions won't always be the same as your classmates' opinions because you may have different interests and hobbies. However, thinking and feeling differently from your classmates is okay. In fact, it allows you to learn from them.

In this activity, you are required to write down your opinions about various topics, then walk around the classroom and ask different classmates what their opinions are on the same topics, and write them down next to yours. The goal is to not ask the same classmate twice, so reach out to different people. After you have filled out all of the squares, go back to your seat and reflect on how differently you think from your classmates. Remember, everyone's opinion is acceptable.

Various topics	My opinion	Classmate's opinion
My favorite food to eat is...		
The school subject I like the most is...		
The school subject I dislike the most is...		
My favorite sport to play is...		
The best cartoon show on TV is...		
My favorite color is...		
The game I like to play the most is...		

Activity 11: Friendship Bracelets

Friendships are the emotional bonds we build with our peers. Friends can make us feel good about ourselves and help us when we are faced with problems.

In this creative activity, you will have an opportunity to create a friendship bracelet for a close friend who may be in your class or who goes to a different school. Your cuddly pets and siblings also count as friends, so your bracelet can be made for them, too! Below are the materials and instructions you will need to create your friendship bracelet.

Materials

- *knitting wool*
- *scissors*
- *an assortment of colorful beads*

Instructions

1. *Unroll the wool and measure it along your wrist to get the right size.*
2. *Add three inches to this measurement, then cut the wool with scissors.*
3. *Tie one bead to one end of the wool to prevent the beads from falling off.*
4. *Thread beads onto the wool, creating a unique pattern with different colors, shapes, and sizes.*
5. *Continue threading beads until you have enough to fit your wrist, leaving about three inches of wool at the end for tying.*

Activity 12: My Coping Strategies

Empathy is not only shown to others but it can also be shown to yourself. When you are having a bad day and need to be comforted, you can show yourself empathy by treating yourself like you would a friend. Healthy coping strategies are behaviors that make you feel better whenever you are upset. It is important to have a few healthy coping strategies that you can turn to during difficult times.

The flash cards below display the different types of coping strategies you can practice when you aren't feeling well. Select your favorite coping strategies, cut them out, and then glue them on the blank page found at the end of this chapter. When you are done, detach the page and hang it up on a wall in the classroom so that you are reminded of what you can do when you are feeling down.

Taking Deep Breaths

Hugging My Favorite Toy

Squeezing a Stress Ball

Counting Up to 10

Drinking Water

Listening to Music

Saying Something Positive

Coloring a Picture

Asking for Help

Thinking of Someone I Love

Eating a Healthy Snack

Taking a Time-Out

Playing My Favorite Game

Activity 13: Journaling About My Highs and Lows

Journaling is a writing practice that allows you to connect with your thoughts and feelings. It involves sharing ideas or writing about events that happen in your life so that you can get your thoughts on paper. Besides improving your writing skills, journaling can help you cope with big emotions and make good decisions about handling tough situations.

In this activity, you are required to complete the following journal prompts to practice sharing your thoughts. Read the prompts carefully and answer to the best of your ability.

1. Describe your favorite childhood memory.

_____

_____

_____

_____

_____

_____

_____

_____

_____

_____

_____

_____

_____

_____

_____

2. Name a person that you care about. What do you love about them?

_____

_____

_____

_____

_____

_____

_____

_____

_____

_____

_____

3. What helps you calm down when you are frightened?

_____

_____

_____

_____

_____

_____

_____

4. What are three things that make you laugh?

_____

_____

_____

_____

_____

_____

_____

_____

_____

_____

_____

_____

5. What's your favorite task to perform at home?

_____

_____

_____

_____

_____

_____

_____

6. What's the best advice you have received from someone?

_____

_____

_____

_____

_____

_____

_____

_____

_____

_____

_____

7. Name three things that you absolutely love about yourself.

_____

_____

_____

_____

_____

_____

_____

8. Who is someone that you miss the most? What would you say to them if they were sitting next to you right now?

_____

_____

_____

_____

_____

_____

_____

_____

_____

_____

_____

9. Do you remember the first day of school? Describe how the day went and how you felt when meeting new people.

_____

_____

_____

_____

_____

_____

_____

10. What are three things you can do to show your friends how much you care about them?

_____

_____

_____

_____

_____

_____

_____

_____

_____

_____

Activity 14: Fun Empathy Board Games

Did you know that playing board games can help you learn to understand how your friends feel? It's true! When you play games with your classmates, you get to practice being kind and taking turns. You also learn how to solve problems and manage your feelings. And guess what? There are so many fun board games about empathy! Here are some ideas that you and your teacher might like to try out together (searchable on the website www.teacherspayteachers.com):

- **Let's Build Empathy Game:** Learn how to build empathy, take different perspectives, and solve social problems with this fun game that includes 160 scenario cards based on real-world situations.

- **Self-Control Speedway:** Practice self-regulation skills by answering 160 questions on healthy coping strategies cards. The aim is to promote a discussion around self-control and practice helpful behaviors.

- **Mindfulness Game:** Learn soothing mindfulness techniques that can help you manage big emotions and feel calm whenever you are overwhelmed. The game includes 130 cards and activities that explore practices like deep breathing and positive affirmations.

Activity 15: Helping Out in the Classroom

Take a look around your beautiful classroom. Imagine how much time and effort it takes to keep your classroom clean and organized. Think about the small jobs that your teacher does before and after school to prepare for your lessons, such as printing papers, tidying the desks, and opening the windows.

For the next week, your task is to help your teacher keep the classroom running effectively by taking on a small job that is suitable for your strengths and abilities. If there aren't a lot of jobs available, your teacher will create a roster and assign different students each week until everyone has been allowed to help out.

Activity 16: Mending a Broken Heart

Words carry the power to help or hurt other people. What you say to others goes through their ears and straight to the heart. They can either feel happiness or sadness after listening to you share your thoughts.

Mending a Broken Heart is a creative activity that shows you the impact of hurtful words. Place a sheet of paper in front of you and trace a big heart with a marker. Feel free to color the heart with red crayons or pencils if you have enough time. Once your heart has been designed, cut it out using a pair of scissors and throw away the scrap paper.

Your teacher will go through a list of words and statements that people sometimes say. If you hear a word or statement that is hurtful, fold a piece of your heart. Continue to listen for more statements. Eventually, your heart will be completely folded after hearing several hurtful words and statements.

Slowly open the folds and straighten out the heart again. Notice all of the crinkles on the heart. These crinkles represent the scars that hurtful words leave on someone's heart. As a class, discuss ways to avoid saying hurtful words and statements to others.

Activity 17: Complimenting Myself

There is nobody else like you in this world, and that is why you are so special! Sometimes, when you are in a crowd full of people, you can forget about the strengths and abilities that make you stand out. This activity serves to remind you of the things you are good at. You may not have the same superpowers as your classmates, but you have your own awesome powers that make you a fascinating individual.

Various topics	What I am good at
School Subjects	
Sports	
House chores	
Friendships	
Hobbies	

Activity 18: Complimenting Others

Everybody has positive qualities and abilities. They may not be the same ones that you possess, but they are equally important and deserve to be appreciated.

In the previous activity, you complimented yourself for the awesome strengths displayed in different areas of your life. For this activity, you are required to get into pairs and compliment a classmate for the things they are good at. They will also be complimenting you for positive things they notice.

Before you start writing, spend 10 minutes interviewing each other so you can learn more about your strengths. Here are some interview questions you can ask each other:

- *What school subject are you really good at?*
- *What hobbies do you enjoy?*
- *What makes you a good friend?*
- *What are the things that make you feel proud to be you?*
- *What house chores do you like the most?*
- *What is your favorite sport to play?*

After you have conducted the interviews, complete the table below based on your classmate's responses. They will also complete a similar table based on your responses.

Various topics	What my classmate is good at
School Subjects	
Sports	
House chores	
Friendships	
Hobbies	

Activity 19: Empathy Storytelling

Here is another writing activity to help you reflect on a time when you have displayed empathy. On a piece of paper, describe a situation from the past where you showed empathy to someone who needed support. Perhaps they were faced with a problem or felt worried about something. Explain how the situation started, unfolded, and ended. Mention some of the choices you made that helped to improve the situation. When the whole class has completed their stories, take turns reading them out loud and sharing your experience with everyone. Use the blank page at the end of the chapter to write your story.

Activity 20: Performing Random Acts of Kindness

You don't need to wait for a special occasion to practice kindness! Being kind is about considering what someone might need and taking action to help them. For example, kindness is seeing a child struggling to get down from the swing set and heading over to help them climb off. Kindness could also be noticing that a classmate is sitting alone on a bench and inviting them to play with you.

For the next few weeks, perform kind and thoughtful behaviors for your classmates. Let your teacher know what you have done so they can write your name on a piece of paper and place it inside a jar. The more acts of kindness that you perform, the more times your name gets to be added to the jar. At the end of the month, your teacher will select a name from the jar and the person they pick will receive a special reward.

Activity 21: Respectfully Disagreeing

When your classmates share their ideas and thoughts, you might shake your head and disagree with what they are saying. This is perfectly normal when you have different thoughts and feelings. Nevertheless, how you express disagreement is important to ensure that you don't hurt the other person's feelings.

In this activity, you will get to practice three ways of disagreeing with your classmates. Get into pairs and create a short skit where both of you disagree on something. Practicing using these statements when disagreeing with each other:

- *I hear what you are saying, but I see things differently.*
- *I have a different opinion. Would you like to hear it?*
- *I understand where you are coming from, but I disagree.*

After performing the skit, gather as a class and discuss how it felt to disagree with your group member, and which phrases you felt comfortable saying.

Activity 22: The Empathy Tree

There are a multitude of ways where you can show empathy to others. The Empathy Tree is a group activity that allows you to brainstorm different ways to practice empathy.

Your teacher will hang up a large cardboard cutout of a tree with empty branches on a classroom wall. Your job is to create leaves out of green paper and write ideas on them about how you can show empathy. Maybe it's listening to a friend when they're sad, or helping someone who's feeling left out. Stick your leaves onto the branches using Sticky Tack, and soon your classroom tree will be covered in all the amazing ways you can all show empathy to each other!

Activity 23: Can You HEAR Me?

Listening to others can be super easy when you all think the same way. But, when you don't agree, listening can feel tricky. That's where our special tool called "HEAR" comes in! HEAR stands for Halt, Engage, Anticipate, and Replay. These are four cool steps that help you listen carefully, even if you don't like what you hear. Below are the instructions for practicing this tool in everyday conversations.

- **H–Halt:** Tell your mind to stop thinking about your own ideas and listen to what the other person is saying.
- **E–Engage:** Turn toward the person and make eye contact. Focus on understanding the words that are coming out of their mouth.
- **A–Anticipate:** Be curious about learning something new. Tell yourself that the message the other person has to share is important and needs your attention.
- **R–Replay:** Play back the other person's message in your mind so that you can make sense of it. If there is something that you don't understand, ask them to repeat their message or explain it differently.

Practice the four HEAR steps with your classmates, role-playing how you would perform them in real-life situations.

Activity 24: Take a Trip Down Memory Lane

In this heartfelt activity, you will get to remember all the positive memories you made as a younger child. Think about all those special moments, like your birthdays, vacations, and times spent with family. Make a special timeline of your childhood on a piece of cardboard paper, starting from when you were little, like 3 years old, all the way until now. So, if you have any old photos at home that show these awesome memories, ask your parents if you can bring them to school.

You can stick your pictures on your timeline using Sticky Tack, and then, you get a chance to stand up in front of the class and share your timeline. Don't forget to tell your classmates about each photo, like where you were and what you were doing. Here are some questions to consider when making your presentation:

- *Who is in the photo?*
- *Where was the photo taken?*
- *What is happening in the photo?*
- *How were you feeling at the time?*

Activity 25: Feeling Masks

In ancient Greece, masks were worn by actors to show the character they were playing. Whenever an actor would portray a different character, they would wear another mask. The masks displayed emotions matching the character's personality. Some masks appeared angry and serious, while others appeared joyful and humorous.

In this activity, you will get an opportunity to create a mask to display your personality. Thereafter, you will be assigned into groups and create a short drama performance based on your characters. The materials and instructions for creating your mask have been provided below.

Materials

- *paper plate*
- *scissors*
- *hole punch*
- *knitting wool*
- *wood glue*
- *accessories (e.g., feathers, pom poms, beads, pipe cleaners, etc.)*
- *craft supplies (e.g., markers, coloring pencils, etc.)*

Instructions

1. *Place a paper plate in front of you and cut it in half to create two semicircles.*
2. *On one semicircle, trace two eyes and a nose with a marker, matching the position of your eyes and nose. Then, cut them out.*
3. *Punch two holes, about 1-2 inches from the sides of the mask.*
4. *Decorate your mask using the provided craft supplies and accessories, creating a design based on your personality.*
5. *Allow the glue to dry for 15-30 minutes if necessary.*
6. *Measure two pieces of string to tie the mask around your face. Thread the strings through the punch holes and make two knots.*
7. *Tie the other ends of the strings around your head.*

Activity 26: Sitting in the Hot Seat

Have you ever been in the hot seat? It happens whenever you are placed in a situation where you need to show vulnerability in front of others. Opening up about your thoughts and feelings can sometimes feel like you are in the hot seat because it makes you feel uncomfortable. However, the benefit is that when you share more about yourself, other people get to discover how amazing you are.

To play this game, your teacher will place a chair in front of the classroom that represents the hot seat. They will ask the class for volunteers who would like to sit in the hot seat and get asked a question about themselves. The question will entail the sharing of opinions, feelings, and personal experiences. The rest of the class needs to pay attention to what is being said, then one person can summarize what they heard afterward. The volunteer should be applauded for their bravery and someone else from the audience can be invited to take the hot seat.

Activity 27: Saying "I'm Sorry" Like a Champion

Sometimes, you will make mistakes and hurt other people's feelings. But the good news is that you can make things better by saying the magical words, "I'm sorry."

However, before you do, it's important to understand why you need to apologize in the first place. This activity walks you through some questions you can ask yourself to empathize with someone whom you have wronged and figure out what you can do to make things right.

Think about a time when you took actions that made someone else cry, feel sad, or get angry, and then answer these questions:

1. What were you feeling when you took actions that hurt someone? For example, you may have been feeling irritated, tired, or frustrated.

_____

_____

_____

_____

_____

_____

_____

_____

_____

_____

2. How do you think your actions made the other person feel? For example, your actions may have made the other person feel excluded, upset, or tearful.

_____

_____

_____

_____

_____

_____

_____

_____

_____

3. What could you have done at the time to improve the situation? For example, you could have walked away, taken deep breaths, or kept quiet to avoid saying hurtful words.

_____

_____

_____

_____

_____

_____

_____

_____

_____

_____

4. Write down the actions that you are sorry for and wish they never happened. For example, you may be sorry for hitting your classmates, grabbing toys, or yelling at your parents.

_____

_____

_____

_____

_____

_____

_____

_____

5. What changes can you make to your behavior to make sure these actions don't happen again? For example, you could learn to count to 10 before opening your mouth to speak or you could report a classmate's behavior to the teacher to get the help you need.

_____

_____

_____

_____

_____

_____

_____

_____

_____

_____

Activity 28: Empathy Rocks!-Classroom Rules for Positive Interactions

Building empathy requires ongoing practice. So, to help you remember what empathy looks like, you can brainstorm and create classroom rules to set achievable standards of behavior.

Sit together around in a circle and take turns making suggestions for rules that promote empathy. Your teacher will be in charge of guiding the conversation, offering tips, and writing down the suggestions you come up with.

In the end, you should agree on a certain number of rules that you can enforce in the classroom. Try not to exceed five rules. Your teacher will create a poster, print it out, and hang up a laminated copy on the wall.

To get your creative brain working, here are some ideas for classroom rules that you can apply:

- Say "please" and "thank you."
- Use kind words when speaking to everyone.
- Check on classmates when they are looking sad.
- Take turns sharing toys and other items with others.
- Listen carefully when other people are speaking.
- Respect other classmates' personal space.
- Follow the advice and instructions given by your teacher.
- Ask for help when you feel confused.
- Say "I'm sorry" when you are in the wrong.

Activity 29: Empathy Alphabet

You can practice different types of empathetic responses by going through your ABCs. Each letter of the empathy alphabet consists of a phrase that demonstrates empathy. Challenge yourself to learn all of the phrases, and practice them at school and home.

A	B	C	D	E	F

Acknowledge others' feelings	**Be patient**	**Consider their point of view**	**Don't judge**	**Encourage them**	**Forgive mistakes**
---	---	---	---	---	---
"I can see that you are sad, and that's okay."	"I am listening to you. Take your time."	"I understand where you are coming from."	"I am curious to learn more from you."	"You did a good job on the project. Well done!"	"I forgive you. Everyone makes mistakes."

G

Give them space

"I will give you time alone to cool down."

H

Help when needed

"Is there something I can do to help you?"

I

Include everyone

"Let us all play together so that nobody is left out."

J

Just listen

"You can talk. I will sit quietly and listen."

K

Kind words matter

"Thank you for being a good friend."

L

Look for nonverbal cues

"I noticed that you are frowning. Are you okay?"

M

Make eye contact

"I am paying attention to what you have to say."

N

Never interrupt

"Please share everything you need to say."

O

Offer support

"I am here if you need someone to talk to."

P

Praise their efforts

"You did well on the test. I am so proud."

Q

Question gently

"Could you please explain this to me again?"

R

Respect their feelings

"Your feelings matter to me."

S

Show that you care

"Can I give you a hug to make you feel better?"

T

Thank them for sharing

"Thank you for opening up to me."

U

Understand their needs

"What would make you feel better right now?"

V

Validate their emotions

"I know this must be tough for you."

W

Wait patiently

"Take your time to express your ideas."

X

eXpress empathy sincerely

"It's okay to be sad. I will be here for you."

Y

Yield to their experiences

"Your experiences are valid and unique."

Z

Zoom in on feelings

"How did the situation make you feel?"

Activity 30: Putting Empathy Into Practice

You may not currently be in a situation where you are required to show empathy, but maybe in the future, you will. The following prompts provide scenarios where you may need to show empathy. Next to each scenario, write down what actions you can take if you are ever placed in those situations.

Real-life scenario	Empathetic actions I could take
When my classmate doesn't understand instructions given by the teacher, I can...	
When I see a child being left out on the playground, I can...	
When someone shares ideas that I don't like, I can...	
When I notice someone looking sad, I can...	
If I hurt my friend's feelings by mistake, I can...	
When my classmate receives a reward for their hard work, I can...	

Cultivating empathy is about seeking to understand other people and learn more about their thoughts and feelings. On the other hand, empathy is also about being kind and patient with yourself when you are going through tough times. With practice, you can develop your empathy skills and build positive relationships.

Use the space below to write down your empathy story based on the instructions given in Activity 19.

Chapter - 3

Second Grade-Self-Regulation Strategies

Our greatest glory is not in never falling, but in rising every time we fall.

- Confucius

Introduction to Self-Regulation

As we grow older, we come across more situations that don't make us feel good. Problems at school and home start piling up, and they're not always easy to fix. For instance, learning tricky subjects, collaborating in groups, making friends, sharing our feelings, or knowing how to act can be tough. But to help us handle all these changes, we can learn an important skill called self-regulation.

Self-regulation means knowing when we are upset and finding good ways to manage our thoughts and feelings so that we don't get overwhelmed. It's like we're taking care of our minds and bodies when things get tough. Instead of just trying to solve the problem, we pay attention to how we're feeling inside and figure out how to make ourselves feel better.

In the classroom, self-regulation can promote positive and healthy behaviors such as:

- *learning to wait patiently while others speak*
- *being open to sharing toys and giving others a turn*
- *finding appropriate ways to express our feelings*
- *soothing ourselves and calming down when we want to explode*
- *focusing on finding solutions instead of complaining about our problems*

The best part about self-regulation skills is that they can also help us solve problems outside of the classroom, whether it is on the playground, in the lineup queue, or at home with our families. They allow us to create personal goals, monitor our progress, and pay attention to how our behaviors affect the people we care about.

Mindfulness and self-regulation go hand in hand. Mindfulness is about focusing your attention on what's happening right now. It's about enjoying the beautiful sights and sounds around us, as well as understanding the thoughts and feelings we're having.

The good news is that several self-regulation strategies promote mindfulness and can be practiced at home and school. We will explore what these strategies are in the activities below.

30 Weeks of Fun: Self-Regulation Activities for Second-Grade Students

Breathe in. Breathe out. The following self-regulation activities are designed to help you manage uncomfortable situations at school and at home so that you can choose how to behave. Get ready to learn new ways to calm yourself down when you are upset and to control your feelings without allowing them to get too big.

Activity 1: Taking Deep Breaths

Breathing is an automatic behavior that comes naturally to you. The speed and rhythm of your breathing change depending on how you are feeling. For instance, when you feel scared or overwhelmed about something, your body reacts by breathing faster, which causes discomfort in your chest. The best part is that you can slow down the speed and rhythm of your breathing by practicing deep breathing exercises.

Here is a simple exercise called nostril breathing that you can practice with the guidance of your teacher.

Instructions
1. *Lift your right or left hand in front of you and make a "stop" sign.*
2. *Place your thumb and index finger on either side of your nose, as if blocking a bad smell.*
3. *Press your thumb gently against one nostril and take a deep breath in through the other nostril.*
4. *Close the opposite nostril with your index finger then lift your thumb.*

5. *Breathe out slowly through the nostril you just released.*
6. *Continue to alternate fingers, breathing in through one nostril and out through the other.*

Activity 2: Listening to Nature Music

Nature sounds like birds chirping, rain pouring, or crashing waves connect you to nature and help you calm down when you are feeling angry or worried. The slow relaxing sounds send messages to your brain, letting it know that you are going to be okay. Hearing these sounds could often also encourage you to spend more time outdoors and develop a positive attitude toward plants, insects, and other animals.

At the end of each day, before packing your bags to go home, listen to at least 10 minutes of nature music. You can decide to either lay your head on your desk or lie down on the ground. Close your eyes and allow the harmony and rhythm of nature to bring ease to your mind and body.

Here are suggestions for a child-friendly nature music playlist (searchable on YouTube):

1. *Rain Sound and Rainforest Animals Sound-Relaxing Sleep by 321 Relaxing - Meditating Relax Clips*
2. *Relax with 20 Minutes of Forest Sounds for Meditation & Stress Relief by Meditations with Nature*
3. *Relaxing Birdsong by the Forest Creek, Nightingale with Blackbird in the Background, Natural by Streaming Birds*

Activity 3: Body Stretching

Stretching is a fun way to listen to your body and see how it feels. When you stretch, you can feel different things happening in your body, like little tingles or tight spots. Moving and stretching can help those uncomfortable feelings go away. After stretching, you might feel happier and full of energy, ready to enjoy the rest of your day. Below are three standing stretches you can do at the start or end of the school day.

Neck Stretch
1. *Stand up straight and position your feet shoulder-width apart.*
2. *Slowly tilt your head to the left, bringing your ear toward your shoulder.*
3. *Stay in this position for 10 counts.*
4. *Return to the starting position.*
5. *Repeat the same sequence, tilting your head to the right side.*
6. *Perform this movement 3 times on each side.*

Side Stretch
1. *Stand straight with both feet touching.*
2. *Lift your right arm toward the sky and extend it over your head to the left side of your body.*

You should feel a pulling sensation on the right side of your upper body.

3. Hold the position for 10 seconds.

4. Repeat the same movement with your left arm, extending it over your head to the right side of your body.

5. Hold the position for 10 seconds.

6. Repeat the movement 3 times on each side.

Hamstring Stretch

1. *Stand straight with both feet together.*
2. *Bend over and reach for your toes with your hands, keeping your legs straight if possible.*
3. *Hold the position for 10 seconds.*
4. *Slowly roll your spine back up to a standing position.*

Activity 4: Mindful Snack Time

Meal times provide a great opportunity for practicing mindfulness. When you are smelling, tasting, chewing, and swallowing food, you can focus on the sensations and flavors in your mouth and how your body feels after each bite.

Mindful Snack Time is an exercise you can play while enjoying your snack. It involves eating slowly so that you can pay attention to the appearance, smell, flavor, and texture of food as it travels from your mouth to your belly. It's important to avoid talking or looking around you during this exercise so that you can stay focused.

Here are a few discussion questions your teacher may ask you after you have eaten your snack:

- *Describe the color, shape, pattern, and texture of the snack.*
- *How did the snack feel brushing against your tongue and mouth?*
- *What sounds did the snack make when you were chewing it?*
- *How did you feel after eating the snack?*

Activity 5: Seated Body Scan

Do you ever get those achy feelings in your body when you're sitting in class? Sometimes, these feelings can make it hard to pay attention to the teacher or join in during class activities.

To reduce the sensation of pain, you practice a technique known as the body scan. It's like giving your body a gentle checkup from head to toe. All you have to do is breathe calmly and focus on each part of your body. If you find any spots that feel a bit uncomfortable, you can send your breath there to help them feel better. The best times to try the body scan are in the morning or afternoon when you need a little break.

Below are instructions that your teacher can walk you through.

Instructions
1. Sit comfortably with your back against the chair and your feet planted on the ground.
2. Drop your shoulders and place your hands on your lap.
3. Take a deep breath in through your nose and out through your mouth, then gently close your eyes.
4. Focus on your face. Inside your head, ask yourself: "How is my face feeling?"
5. Notice any sensations. If you feel any discomfort, imagine sending your breath to your face to relax your muscles.
6. Bring your attention to your neck. Ask yourself how it feels. If you notice any tension, send your breath there to help it feel better.
7. Move to your shoulders, back, arms, chest, belly, and so on, asking how each part feels and sending your breath to any areas of discomfort.
8. Continue this sequence until you get to your toes.
9. Once you've scanned your entire body, take a deep breath, then slowly open your eyes.

Activity 6: Explore Your Senses Through Play

Did you know that playing with toys and objects that are bright, squishy, bumpy, soft, tickly, or loud can help you feel better when you're upset? This is because focusing on how these things feel can take your mind off what is bothering you.

In this activity, your teacher will put different sensory toys and objects into a sealed shoebox with a hand-sized opening. When the box comes to you, reach inside and pick one item. Spend some time playing with it and noticing how it looks and feels. You can also trade items with your classmates to experience different sensations.

Some of the items that you may find in the box include:
- a stress ball
- feathers
- pom-poms
- magnetic balls
- Velcro strips
- scented sachets
- pipe cleaner craft objects
- bubble wrap

Activity 7: Take a Mental Health Break

Mental health breaks are short segments throughout the school day where you get to pause work and relax your mind. During mental health breaks, you can practice soothing exercises that can help you feel calm and energized such as going for a walk, having a sip of water, taking deep breaths, or stretching your body. Your teacher will set a timer and announce how much time you have to take a mental health break. When the time is up, return to your seat and continue working on your tasks.

Activity 8: Stop, Think, Act

Self-regulation is about thinking carefully about your options before taking action. The words STOP, THINK, and ACT can help you remember this.

First, use Play-Doh to make these three words on your desk. Then, explain to a classmate what these words mean to you. Afterward, your teacher will ask everyone to talk about what these words mean and how we can use them in real-life situations.

Activity 9: Mirror, Mirror

You can tell your body what to do, and it will listen to you! Mirror, Mirror is a fun game that shows you how much control you have over your body.

Pair up with a classmate and stand facing each other. One of you will be the "mind," and the other will be the "body." The "mind" will make funny faces and silly movements, and the "body" will copy them exactly.

This game helps you see that your mind and body work together. With your thoughts and ideas, you can tell your body to do good things and show positive behaviors.

Activity 10: Speaking Positively to Yourself

One of the ways to cheer yourself up when you're feeling down is to say positive words about yourself. These words help you feel motivated to seek help and pick yourself up again.

Think of yourself as your very own cheerleader! Whenever something is hard or you make a mistake, let that cheerleader inside you say words to lift you up. You can use a simple phrase like "I am" followed by all the cool things about you. For example, if you're working on something tricky, you can say, "I am smart, and I can do this!" And when you're meeting new friends, you can say, "I am kind and friendly." You're awesome, and it's important to remind yourself of that.

Here are more positive statements that you can use to cheer yourself on:

- *I am brave like a lion and can face my fears.*
- *I am creative and can imagine cool ideas.*

- *I am unique and possess many wonderful talents.*
- *I am kind and enjoy making new friends.*
- *I am a hard worker and stay focused in class.*
- *I am loved and supported by my close friends and family.*

Activity 11: Visualize Your Happy Place

If you ever feel like you need to get away from things for a little while, you can imagine your happy place. This can be a real place you've visited in the past or a place you have read about in a book or seen in a movie. Your happy place is where you feel calm and happy. Maybe it's your grandma's house, the zoo or aquarium, a place from your favorite movie, or a sunny beach you've visited before.

To visit your happy place, get comfy in your seat and close your eyes. Imagine you're being lifted and taken to your happy place. Picture yourself walking towards it and feeling excited as you get closer.

Step inside and look around. What do you see? Who is there? What sounds do you hear? What fun things can you do? Explore your happy place for a few minutes and feel yourself getting lighter and happier. When you're ready to come back, take a deep breath and open your eyes.

Activity 12: Body Rocking

Rocking your body back and forth is a great way to feel better. The gentle motion helps you relax and feel calm. Rocking can also help you stay seated in class when you feel like standing up. You get to move without leaving your chair!

To practice body rocking, stretch your arms wide open and give yourself a big hug. Then, slowly rock forward and backward at a pace that feels good to you. You can close your eyes and say kind words to yourself to feel even more comforted.

Activity 13: Weighing Your Choices

In every situation, you can choose how to act. Your choices can make things better or worse.

Weighing Your Choices is a game that helps you learn how to make good choices about what you do. In the table below, you will see real-life scenarios. Write down two choices for each one: one that makes things better and one that makes things worse.

After you finish the worksheet, your teacher will start a classroom discussion about your answers. Listen to what your classmates wrote and think about whether you would make the same choices.

Real-life scenarios	Good choice	Bad choice
During a group project, you notice that one of your classmates isn't participating.		
You've mistakenly forgotten your homework at home and your teacher is asking for it.		
A friend mistakenly spills their juice on your T-shirt.		
You see a child being teased on the playground.		
One of your classmates asks for help to explain the teacher's instructions.		
You are unhappy about the low test score you received for an assignment.		

Activity 14: Have You Reached Your Boiling Point?

Everyone gets angry sometimes—so angry they feel like they might explode! But before we reach that point, our emotions build up step by step. For example, feeling confused might turn into feeling scared, then frustrated, and finally, really angry. By using an emotions thermometer, you can see how close you are to getting angry and choose to calm down instead.

Making an emotions thermometer is easy! Take a sheet of cardboard paper and place it down vertically. Draw a big thermometer outline. If you need help, just ask your teacher. On one side of the thermometer, draw a scale from 1 to 10. On every second number, write these categories:

- *calm, relaxed, peaceful*
- *content, happy, confident*
- *uneasy, confused, uncomfortable*
- *upset, overwhelmed, irritable*
- *angry, jealous, disapproving*

Use colored pencils to color each section, with the colors getting warmer as you go up, like blue, green, yellow, orange, and red. Hang your thermometer in the classroom or take it home and put it on your bedroom wall. Whenever you feel emotional, look at your thermometer to see where you are. Then, take steps to help yourself calm down.

Activity 15: Emotions Detective

You have a special mission as an emotion detective! This week, pretend you're wearing a detective hat and carry a special notebook. Pay close attention to your feelings throughout the day. Whenever your feelings change, write down what you're feeling, what happened to make you feel that way, and how you can react in a positive way.

At the end of the chapter, you'll find a special log sheet to help you keep track of your emotions. Have fun on your detective adventure!

Activity 16: Calm-Down Kit

Sometimes the classroom can get really busy, and you might feel overwhelmed. Instead of fidgeting in your seat or feeling more and more upset, you can find a quiet spot and use your calm-down kit. This kit is a box filled with comforting toys and objects that help you manage strong emotions. When you see or play with these items, you feel happier and more relaxed.

You can make your own calm-down kit in class. Start with an old shoebox and decorate it with craft supplies to make it special. Bring a few small items from home that you can keep in your box perma----

nently. These should be things that make you feel better when you are sad or upset. Find a safe place in the classroom to store your box so you can use it whenever you need to calm down.

Here are examples of the types of items you can include in your calm-down kit:
- *bottle of bubbles*
- *puzzles*
- *fidget cube*
- *small stuffed animal*
- *photo of a pet*
- *small notebook and pen*
- *coloring book and pencils*
- *handwritten note from a loved one*

Activity 17: Behavior Traffic Light

Do you remember the three colors on a traffic light? They are red, yellow, and green. Red means STOP. Yellow means BE CAREFUL. Green means GO.

When you want to tell your classmates what behaviors you like and don't like, you can use the traffic light colors. Red behaviors are mean and hurtful and need to STOP right away. Yellow behaviors make you feel uncomfortable and need to be changed. Green behaviors make you happy, and you enjoy them.

In the table below, write down some behaviors that match these three colors. As a class, talk about different ways to tell others when they should stop, be careful, or go ahead with their behaviors. Think about how to use words and body language to share your messages.

Red Behaviors RED = STOP!	Yellow Behaviors YELLOW = BE CAREFUL!	Green Behaviors GREEN = GO!

Activity 18: Emotion Freeze Tag

It's time to head outside and play freeze tag-with a fun twist!

Spread out on the field and run away from the person who is "It." If you get tagged, you have to freeze right where you are. Your teacher will then ask you to share a story about a time you felt a certain emotion, like happy, sad, or excited. After you share your story, you become "It," and the game continues.

What's great about this game is that it helps you learn more about your feelings and how to accept them, which shows you that you can have fun and learn at the same time!

Activity 19: Breathing Buddy

A quick and easy way to calm down is to take deep belly breaths. To help you do this, you will need a breathing buddy. You can bring a small stuffed animal from home or grab a small book from the classroom bookshelf. This will be your breathing buddy whenever you want to practice belly breathing.

Find a spot on the floor and lie down facing the ceiling. Place the stuffed animal or book on your belly. Take a deep breath through your nose and let it out through your mouth. When you breathe in, your breathing buddy should rise with your belly. When you breathe out, your breathing buddy should fall with your belly. Repeat this exercise several times.

Activity 20: Breathing Straw Activity

Do you want to try a fun breathing exercise? Grab a straw and a small piece of tissue paper. Place the tissue paper on the table in front of you. Now, take a deep breath and blow through the straw to lift the tissue paper into the air. Try to keep it floating by taking slow, deep breaths through the straw. Remember to breathe from your belly and blow out slowly. After a few tries, take a break and breathe normally. Notice how you feel after the exercise.

Activity 21: Creating Your Classroom Calm-Down Corner

Take a look around your classroom. Is there a spot that could become a cozy calm-down corner? Having a calm-down corner means that you have a special place to go when you need a break from sitting at your desk or just want some time to think and breathe.

Making a calm-down corner takes careful planning and teamwork. As a class, you need to choose the best spot for this corner and decide which toys, objects, and comfy furniture to add to make it feel relaxing. You will also need to set some rules for the calm-down corner, like staying quiet and not talking to other kids so everyone can relax. Once you have a plan, show it to your teacher, who will help you set it up.

Activity 22: Five Senses Check-In

When you have lots of thoughts zooming around in your head and it's hard to focus on your school work, take a deep breath and remind yourself to stay in the present moment. Play the Five Senses Check-In game by looking around the classroom and noticing what you can see, hear, smell, touch, and taste. Turn it into a fun challenge by finding five things you can see, four things you can hear, three things you can smell, two things you can touch, and one thing you can taste. At the end of the game, see how you're feeling. Have your thoughts slowed down?

Activity 23: Practicing Asking for Help

When you ask your friends and teachers for help, it's super cool! It helps you understand what you need to do to finish your work or solve problems. To make sure you ask for help the right way, it's good to practice how you might talk to someone like a teacher. Let's try a fun activity to get better at this!

Find a partner and get ready to role-play. Think of a situation where a student has a problem and needs help from the teacher. Act out the positive conversation that can be had between the student and the teacher.

Here are conversation suggestions you can consider:
- *Miss Trudy, do you have a moment to speak? I would like to ask you a question.*
- *Miss Trudy, I am struggling with [describe the problem]. Would it be okay to come to your desk later for help?*
- *Miss Trudy, I heard your instructions, but I still don't understand [describe you concern].*
- *Miss Trudy, could you please give me advice on how to handle this situation in the best way?*

After the first skit, switch roles and create another short skit where the student asks the teacher for help. By practicing, you will get better at asking for help in a polite and respectful way!

Activity 24: Mandala Drawing

A mandala is like a magical picture that helps turn sad feelings into happy ones! It's made of lots of cool shapes and designs, all filled with bright rainbow colors. Today, you get to make your very own mandala.

Use your imagination to pick your favorite colors and create beautiful artwork. Remember to stay inside the lines and concentrate on your drawing to feel calm and peaceful. While you color, you can think about times when you turned a sad moment into a happy one.

When you are ready, you can find your mandala to color at the end of the chapter!

Activity 25: The Worry Jar

We all have thoughts that make us feel worried. Maybe it's about homework, or friends, or things we like to do, or stuff that is coming up soon. But if we let those thoughts take over, they can make it hard to focus on what we're doing or enjoy the fun stuff around us.

That's where the worry jar comes in! It's a special container that stays at school or home, and it's just for those worrying thoughts. Whenever you have a worrying thought, tear a piece of paper and write down what the thought is. Then, put it in the jar.

Later, when you're feeling calmer, you can take out the note and read it. Ask yourself: Can I fix this by myself, or do I need some help? If you can fix it, go for it! If you need help, talk to someone you trust.

Activity 26: Personalized Coping Cards

Coping cards are like little helpers that remind you that you're strong and can handle anything that comes your way. They tell you to take deep breaths, to think about what you're good at, and to remember to take care of yourself. It's like having a friendly big brother or sister with you all the time, ready to cheer you up when you're feeling down.

To make your own coping cards, start by writing down good things that help you feel better when things are tough. Then, write those things on the cards below and cut them out. You can keep them in your desk or backpack so you can use them whenever you need a boost.

To feel better, I can...

To feel better, I can...

To feel better, I can...

To feel better, I can...

To feel better, I can...

To feel better, I can...

To feel better, I can...

To feel better, I can...

To feel better, I can...

To feel better, I can...

Activity 27: Guess the Animal Sounds

Gather together on the floor around your teacher and play a fun game called Guess the Animal Sounds! You will listen to recordings of different animals and try to guess which one it is. When you hear a sound, raise your hand and share your guess with the class. But remember, you need to listen carefully and be patient before guessing. Here's a video with some animal sounds for you to practice with: *[www.youtube.com/watch?v=q8emJyUvI6g]*. Have fun guessing together!

Activity 28: Mindful Handwriting

Writing is like a fun game that can make you feel peaceful inside. When you have some extra time in class, you can have fun writing happy words on a blank page.

In this game, copy the happy words in the boxes below. Take your time and use your pencil to trace each letter carefully. Feel how smooth and soft the pencil is as you make each letter. Enjoy making the shapes of the letters!

You are amazing

Dream big

You can do it

Smile often

Believe in yourself

You're unique

You make me laugh

Love yourself

Be brave

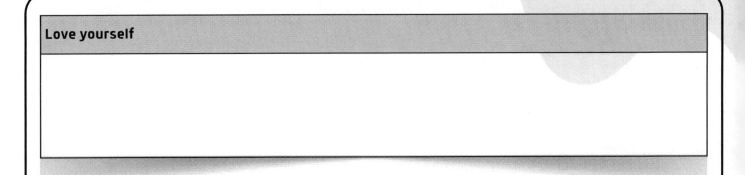

Activity 29: Relaxation Storytime

At the end of the day, when you're feeling tired and you're excited to go home, it's nice to have a peaceful storytime. This week, your teacher will finish each day by playing a cozy story that will help you relax after all your hard work.

Find a comfy spot in front of your teacher. If there's room, you can even lie down. Close your eyes and open your ears to listen carefully as your teacher plays the audiobook. Imagine the gentle words and pictures in your mind. Here are some story suggestions your teacher might choose from (searchable on YouTube):

- *Broken Crayons Still Color by Toni Collier (YouTube account: Reading Robinsons)*
- *Let's Say Goodnight to 30 Farm Animals by Moonbeam Tales (YouTube account: Moonbeam Tales)*
- *I am Jellyfish by Ruth Paul (YouTube account: Kiwi Kids Books)*

Activity 30: Write Your Happy Song

When you're feeling sad, do you ever hum or sing? Music can make you dance, and it can also cheer you up on tough days. Instead of singing a song you already know, try making up your own happy song to lift your spirits. Your song should be no longer than 10 lines and must include kind words that make you feel better and stronger. If you feel brave, you can sing your song for the class to help everyone feel happy too!

Practicing self-regulation skills with fun and interactive activities like these can help you stay strong when things change or go wrong at school and home. In the end, you'll feel more in control of your thoughts, feelings, and actions.

_____

_____

_____

_____

_____

_____

_____

_____

_____

_____

_____

_____

_____

_____

_____

Use the log sheet below to record and keep track of your emotions based on the instructions given in Activity 15.

What are you feeling?	What happened to make you feel that way?	How can you respond in a positive way?

Use the space below to color in the mandala represented below based on the instructions given in Activity 24.

Chapter - 4

Third Grade-Nurturing Healthy Relationships

Nobody can go back and start a new beginning, but anyone can start today and make a new ending.
- Maria Robinson

Understanding Healthy Relationships

Relationships are special connections we have with people like our parents, siblings, friends, and teachers. Each relationship is unique, because we bond with each person in different ways. For example, we play and have fun with friends, while we respect and appreciate teachers for their support even though we don't play with them.

Healthy relationships are like sunshine on a rainy day-they bring out the best in us, making us feel happy, energized, and safe. On the flip side, unhealthy relationships are like dark clouds-they bring out the worst in us, making us feel scared, judged, and left out. Our aim at home and school should be to nurture more healthy relationships, filling our lives with people who lift us and help us shine brighter every day.

Building healthy relationships takes effort. Our goal is to understand others by imagining what they might need or appreciate. Additionally, we need to be brave enough to speak up, share our thoughts, ask questions, express feelings, and show kindness.

Remembering all this might seem like a big task, so here are five rules that sum up the secrets to lasting, healthy relationships:

1. *Respect one another.*
2. *Honesty is the best policy.*
3. *Check on one another.*
4. *Balance give and take.*
5. *Kind words matter.*

Now that you know the rules of healthy relationships, it's time to put them into practice by completing the following 30 activities over the next 30 weeks. Are you up for the challenge?

Let's go!

30 Weeks of Fun: Relationship-Building Activities for Third-Grade Students

You deserve relationships that bring joy to your heart and inspire you to grow! To cultivate these special connections, it's important to learn how to be a supportive friend and express yourself with confidence. Here are 30 fun and imaginative activities to help you enhance your skills in building meaningful relationships.

Activity 1: Creating a Friendship Web

Friendship can mean different things to different people, and this activity is a chance to explore those differences. By hearing what being a good friend means to others, you might discover new ideas you hadn't considered before.

To play this game, gather in a circle with your classmates. One person starts by sharing their thoughts on friendship and then rolls a ball of yarn to someone else in the circle. The next person catches the yarn and shares their definition of friendship before passing it to another classmate. Keep passing the yarn around, ensuring that it doesn't go to the same person twice. By the end, you'll have created a web of diverse perspectives on friendship.

Activity 2: Greetings and Farewells

Saying "hello!" and "goodbye!" to your teachers and classmates every day is more than just a polite routine-it's a powerful way to show you care. It's your chance to let them know they matter, even if you don't talk much during the day.

Greetings and Farewells is a special game we play at the beginning and end of each day. In the morning, when you see your teachers and friends, greet them warmly and ask how they're doing. And when the day ends, say goodbye with a smile, sharing something you're excited about when you get home. And hey, if you want to add in some fun gestures like high-fives, fist bumps, or secret handshakes, go ahead! It's all about spreading positivity and making connections.

Activity 3: Listening Pairs

To have meaningful conversations with your classmates, it's important to practice listening without interrupting. If that seems challenging, don't worry! Listening Pairs is a game designed to help you become a better listener.

Grab a ruler and stand facing your partner. Take turns speaking and listening. The speaker holds the ruler while talking, and then passes it to the listener, who responds. The task of the listener is to show they're paying attention by doing gestures like eye contact, nodding, or smiling–no words are allowed. To respond, the listener must take the ruler from the speaker and share their thoughts. This back-and-forth is repeated until the conversation has ended.

Activity 4: Fun Facts

How often do you chat with your classmates about what they enjoy doing? You might be amazed at the cool talents and hobbies they have! Asking questions isn't just a way to start conversations, but it's also a way to keep them going.

This activity gets you moving and mingling in class. Talk to as many classmates as you can and write down the new things you learn about them on a sheet. The catch? Only write down stuff you didn't know before. For instance, if you already know your friend's pet dog is named Betty, don't write it down. But if they share something fresh like loving the color orange, that's worth noting. By the end, you'll have a neat list of fun facts about your classmates!

Here are a list of questions you can use to get the conversations started:
- *What's your favorite food?*
- *What do you enjoy doing on the weekends?*
- *Who do you admire most in your life?*
- *What is your favorite school subject?*
- *What is your worst school subject?*
- *What's your favorite game to play?*
- *What do you hope to be when you grow up?*
- *What is something that you are really good at?*

- *If you could travel anywhere in the world, where would you go?*
- *What movie or TV show can you watch repeatedly without getting bored?*

Activity 5: Empathy Role-Play

It's time to practice handling different social situations with your classmates. Your teacher will pair you up and give you a common social scenario to role-play in two ways: the right way and the wrong way. Spend 10 minutes planning your skits, then take turns presenting them to the class. Don't reveal which skits show the right or wrong responses-let your classmates guess!

Here are some scenarios you may be required to role-play:
- *sharing a toy*
- *apologizing for a mistake*
- *asking to join a group activity*
- *responding to a hurtful comment*
- *helping a classmate in need*
- *accepting a compliment*
- *responding to being left out of a game*
- *reaching a compromise with a friend*

Activity 6: Reading Together

Taking turns is a great way to show your classmates that you care about them. You can practice this behavior in different social situations, like playing games, having conversations, or working on group projects.

In this activity, you will practice taking turns with a classmate by reading a book together. Each of you will read a short paragraph, then let the other person take their turn reading a paragraph. While your classmate is reading, follow along and listen carefully. To make the reading fun, you can use silly voices!

Activity 7: Lineup Mingling

Do you want to play a game called Lineup Mingling? For the rest of the week, your teacher will give you different ways to line up before class. For example, she might ask you to line up by your birthdays, starting from January 1st to December 31st. Another day, she might ask you to line up by height, from shortest to tallest, or by the first letter of your name. You will need to talk with your classmates to find your place and get into the correct order. The best part is that you will learn new and interesting things about your classmates that you may not have known before!

Activity 8: Friendship Recipe

Form small groups with your classmates. Create a recipe for the ideal friendship. Discuss and list the qualities of a good friend. These are your "ingredients." Think of things like kindness, honesty, trust, and fun.

Write down the steps to building a friendship. These are your "cooking instructions." Consider steps like sharing, listening, spending time together, and helping each other. Combine your ingredients and cooking instructions to create a Friendship Recipe. Make sure it's clear and easy to understand.

Take turns standing in front of the class and presenting your Friendship Recipe to everyone. Explain why you chose each ingredient and step.

_____

_____

_____

_____

_____

_____

_____

_____

_____

_____

_____

_____

_____

Activity 9: Common Denominator

Everyone has their own unique qualities and interests, but you also share some with your classmates. This game helps you discover those similarities! **Here's how to play:**

1. *Your teacher will start a timer for five minutes.*
2. *Get into small groups.*
3. *Go through a set of questions to learn about each other's likes and dislikes.*

In the space below, write down all the things you have in common, like your favorite games, foods, seasons, and more. Flip to the end of the chapter to color in the flag with colors, symbols, and drawings that represent your shared qualities and interests.

_____

_____

_____

_____

_____

_____

_____

_____

_____

_____

_____

_____

_____

_____

Activity 10: Thank-You Notes

When people treat us kindly and help us when we're in trouble, it's important to thank them for their kindness.

Think about times when your classmates did something that made you smile, like when someone remembered to say "happy birthday" on your special day or when someone asked if you were okay when you felt sad. Write down five thank-you notes for five different people in your class. You can thank your teachers, too, since they are always there to help you. Cut out your thank-you notes and deliver them to the right people.

To:

Thank you for:

To:

Thank you for:

To:

Thank you for:

To:
Thank you for:

To:
Thank you for:

Activity 11: Knock, Knock, Who Am I?

How well do you know the sounds of your classmates' voices?

In this fun game, everyone sits in a circle, and one person sits blindfolded in a chair in the middle. When the game starts, everyone needs to stay quiet. The teacher will point to someone sitting around the circle. That person will quietly stand up, go behind the blindfolded person, and say, "Knock, knock, who am I?"

The blindfolded person has three chances to guess who is behind them. After each guess, the teacher will say "Yes" if they're right or "No" if they're wrong. After the third guess, the blindfolded person can take off the blindfold and see who it is. Then, someone else gets a turn to be blindfolded in the middle. Keep playing until everyone has had a chance to be blindfolded.

Activity 12: Marshmallow Tower

Three brains working together to solve problems are better than one! Teamwork lets you share ideas and learn from others, making it easier to tackle challenges.

Here's a fun challenge that requires a team effort–it's called Marshmallow Tower. You'll get a bag of marshmallows (try not to eat any!) and toothpicks. Your task is to build the tallest structure you can, using only these two items. The tower needs to stand on its own for at least a minute without collapsing. Before you start building, spend 10 minutes brainstorming and drawing your structure on paper to see how it would look.

Activity 13: Feasting on Culture

Every student in the classroom has a unique story about where they come from, and this can be shared through their culture and values. Feasting on Culture is an exciting activity that invites you to explore new flavors and traditions.

Each student should bring a snack or dish that is important in their culture. During a short presentation, you will explain what the snack or dish is, how it's prepared, and when it's usually eaten. After everyone has presented, place all the food items on a table and enjoy sharing them together.

Activity 14: Alphabet Trivia

Build connections with your classmates by playing a fun game of Alphabet Trivia. In groups, work together to think of words that start with each letter of the alphabet based on a topic your teacher gives you. For example, if the topic is "food," you might come up with:

- **A**: Apple
- **B**: Beans
- **C**: Carrots
- **D**: Donuts
- **E**: Eggplant

The first group to complete the alphabet wins! If there's time, you can play again with a new topic like animals, countries, or household items.

Activity 15: Friendship Book Club

Listen to an audiobook about friendship and discuss it as a class, exploring the characters' relationships and the lessons learned about friendship. Imagine that you were the character and think about what you would have done in their situation.

Here are some friendship-themed books that you can listen to online (searchable on YouTube):
- *The Choices I Make: Self-Regulation Skills by Michael Gordon (YouTube account: Read Well)*
- *Our Class is a Family by Shannon Olsen (YouTube account: Ms. Michelle's Storytime)*
- *The Buddy Bench by Patty Brozo (YouTube account: Reading Time)*

Activity 16: Taking Care of the Classroom

Helping others is a great way to build strong relationships and show how much you care. In this activity, your job is to help your teacher take care of the classroom by doing small tasks like handing out papers, picking up trash, wiping desks, or taking attendance. If there aren't enough tasks for everyone, you can work in pairs. At the end of the week, the whole class will get a reward for being generous helpers!

Activity 17: Solving Friendship Dilemmas

Relationships aren't always easy. Even best friends can have disagreements sometimes. But there are positive ways to handle friendship problems and get back to a happy place with your classmates.
Get into groups and discuss how you would solve the following friendship dilemmas. For each solution, write down the pros and cons.

Your friend keeps teasing you about something that makes you feel uncomfortable. How can you tell them to stop without hurting their feelings?
Suggestion:
Pros and Cons:

You are working in a group with a classmate that you don't like very much. How can you work together and get the job done without fighting?

Suggestion:

Pros and Cons:

Your friend wants you to do something that goes against your classroom rules. What can you do to stand up for yourself?

Suggestion:

Pros and Cons:

Activity 18: 30-Second Introduction

Imagine meeting new classmates for the first time. You might feel a mix of excitement and nerves, wondering what to say. Do you talk about your siblings, favorite foods, or hobbies? There's so much about you to share, but introductions need to be brief.

So, here's a fun challenge: Write a short paragraph introducing yourself to someone new. Include 3-5 interesting facts you want them to know. Keep it short and sweet to leave them curious for more. Take your introduction home and practice saying it with a warm smile in front of a mirror. You never know when you might need to introduce yourself soon!

Activity 19: Traffic Light Zones

When people get too close to your body, it can make you feel uncomfortable. You can use a helpful idea called the traffic light system to let them know if they're standing or sitting too close.

Imagine it like this: If they are a arm's length away, they are in the green zone, which is good. If they come closer-close enough to touch you-that's the orange zone. It might still feel okay, depending on who it is. But if they get so close that you can smell their breath, that's the red zone, and they need to step back. You can practice this idea with a friend in a role-play and find ways to politely ask them to give you some space.

Activity 20: Friendship Pledge

To nurture strong and lasting friendships, it's important to consistently show respect and kindness to your friends. Whether they're feeling sad and need someone to lean on or whether they're bursting with excitement, being there for them is key.

A friendship pledge is a special promise you make to your friends, pledging to always be there for them. It lists the little things you're committed to doing to make them happy.

At the end of this chapter, you will find a blank friendship pledge that you can customize for a dear friend. Once you've filled it out, tear the page and give it to them as a tangible reminder of your dedication to their happiness.

Activity 21: Gratitude Circle

Gather in a circle with your classmates and take turns sharing something nice that someone did for you lately. It could be as simple as a warm smile in the morning, lending a hand with your schoolwork, or standing up for you on the playground. You can also thank your teacher for being supportive and helpful recently.

Activity 22: Friendship Quilt

True friendship is all about embracing each other's differences. A friendship quilt is a magical blanket made of many colorful fabrics sewn together. Each piece represents the special qualities that make us who we are.

Now, you can help create your own class quilt! Your teacher will give you patches of fabric. Use a black marker to sign your name on your patch and, if there is space, share your favorite quote. Your teacher will sew all the patches together, and soon you will have your shared quilt to use in class!

Activity 23: Collaborative Storywriting

Working together on projects with your classmates sparks more creativity. In this activity, you will team up to create a story about friendship.

Work together in small groups, and choose someone to start the story with an opening line like, "Once upon a time, there were two best friends..." Then, pass around the paper, with each person adding a short paragraph, about three lines long, to the story. Use different colored pens so that you can see everyone's ideas come together. If your story needs more space, ask for another sheet of paper, but try not to go over two pages.

Now for the best part-nominate someone to read the story to the class, or take turns reading the parts you wrote. It's up to you!

Activity 24: Classroom Awards

A great way to show appreciation to classmates who help others is by giving them awards! On a piece of paper, write down the names of a few classmates who you think deserve awards in the following categories:

1. **Best Listener:** *Always ready to lend an ear and listen with care*
2. **Most Supportive:** *Constantly offering help and encouragement to classmates*
3. **Kindness Champion:** *Regularly showing kindness through actions and words*
4. **Team Player:** *Excelling in working well with others and promoting teamwork*
5. **Conflict Resolver:** *Skilled at helping friends work through disagreements peacefully*

Remember, you can't nominate yourself for these awards, only your friends. But don't be sad if you don't get chosen this time! These awards can be given every month or every few months, so everyone will have a chance to win an award eventually!

Activity 25: Personal Growth Timeline

Over the years, you've become more confident in expressing your feelings, controlling your behaviors, and starting conversations with others. The Personal Growth Timeline is a fun activity to see how much you've grown.

Draw a line across the middle of a sheet of paper. Make four big marks on the line for kindergarten, first grade, second grade, and third grade. Under each mark, write about how you used to handle social situations:

- **Kindergarten:** *Maybe you were a shy boy or girl who found it hard to talk to people.*
- **First Grade:** *Maybe you started to make a few friends and felt a bit more comfortable.*
- **Second Grade:** *Maybe you became more talkative and enjoyed playing with your classmates.*
- **Third Grade:** *Maybe you're now a bubbly and confident boy or girl who loves talking to people.*

When you are done, look at your timeline and notice how much you have improved. Pat yourself on the back for learning and practicing relationship-building skills. Great job!

Activity 26: Friendship Bingo

Let's play a game of Friendship Bingo with special cards that show the different qualities of a good friend! Each laminated bingo card will have 9-12 blocks and include qualities like:

- *speaks politely*
- *offers help*
- *takes turns*
- *listens carefully*
- *plays fair*
- *tells the truth*

Once everyone has their card, hold a marker and get ready to check off the qualities you see on your card. When you have checked off three or four qualities in a row (vertically, horizontally, or diagonally), shout "Bingo!" to get your teacher's attention so she can verify your answers. If there's time, swap cards with a classmate and play another round!

Activity 27: Reflection Journal

Here's a fun activity you can start at school and finish at home if you need more time. It's called reflection journaling, and it's a way to write about your past memories and learn important lessons from them. This can help you understand yourself better, letting you figure out why you act the way you do.

For this activity, think back to the good and bad times you've had with friends. When you write about these experiences, include how you felt at the time and what you learned from them. Here are two examples:

- **Bad Memory:** One day, I forgot my stationery kit at home, and I felt really worried. Luckily, a friend of mine kindly lent me pens and pencils for the day. From this, I learned that true friends are there to help you when you're in a tough spot.
- **Good Memory:** I'll always cherish the day I met John. We quickly realized we shared lots of interests, and our friendship grew from there. This taught me that being open and sharing with others can lead to amazing friendships.

Activity 28: Collaborative Artwork

Sit in a circle and pass around a large sheet of paper. Each person should add a small drawing, symbol, or phrase that reminds them of friendship before passing the paper to the next person. By the end, you'll have a unique art piece that celebrates friendship, which can be hung up on the classroom wall.

Another fun way to celebrate friendship is by doing hand painting. Each person paints the palm of their left or right hand with a color, then presses their hand onto the sheet of paper. In the end, you will have a colorful artwork made with everyone's handprints.

Activity 29: Friendship Affirmations

Take a moment to think about the kind of friend you are to your classmates. What do you do really well? Where can you improve?

In this activity, you will write friendship affirmations to remind yourself to be a good friend. Affirmations are positive statements that celebrate your strengths and potential. Create between 5 to 10 affirmations that you can post in your homework diary so that you can read them regularly. Here are some examples of what you might write:

- *I am a kind and caring friend.*
- *I listen to my friends and support them.*
- *I am patient and understanding.*
- *I share and take turns with others.*
- *I help my friends when they need it.*
- *I am respectful and considerate.*
- *I encourage my friends to do their best.*
- *I communicate my feelings honestly.*
- *I include everyone in activities.*
- *I apologize when I make a mistake and learn from it.*

Activity 30: Friendship Role Models

When you think of the best example of a good friend, which movie or cartoon characters come to mind? Think about the qualities they exhibit that make them a good friend.

This activity will help you find positive role models who show what it means to be a good friend. Your task is to identify at least two characters you admire for their friendship skills. For each one, answer the following reflection questions:

1. How does this character show that they care about their friends?

_____

_____

_____

_____

_____

_____

_____

_____

_____

_____

_____

_____

_____

_____

_____

_____

_____

2. How does this character make their friends laugh and have fun?

_____

_____

_____

_____

_____

_____

_____

_____

3. What does this character do to show that they are a good listener?

_____

_____

_____

_____

_____

_____

_____

_____

4. How does this character help their friends when they are in trouble or feeling sad?

_____

_____

_____

_____

_____

_____

_____

_____

_____

5. How does this character handle arguments or disagreements with friends?

_____

_____

_____

_____

_____

_____

_____

_____

_____

_____

_____

6. Can you think of a time when you acted like this character to help a friend? What happened?

_____

_____

_____

_____

_____

_____

_____

_____

_____

_____

Healthy relationships inside and outside the classroom aren't built in a day. They need patience and regular care. Keep practicing activities like these to improve your relationship-building skills and have better interactions with others!

Use the space below to color in the flag representing your shared qualities and interests with classmates, based on the instructions given in Activity 9.

Fill out the friendship pledge below based on the instructions given in Activity 20.

<u>My Friendship Pledge</u>

I, _____, pledge to be a good friend who:

1.

_____

_____

_____

2.

_____

_____

_____

3.

_____

_____

_____

4.

_____

_____

_____

_____

5.

_____

_____

_____

_____

_____

Signature: _____

Date: _____

Chapter - 5

Fourth Grade-Cultivating Resilience

Great works are performed not by strength but by perseverance.

- Samuel Johnson

Understanding Resilience

Sometimes, we face tough situations at school and home. These tough times might make us feel sad or worried, but they don't have to bring us down.

Being resilient means staying strong and not giving up, even when things are hard. It helps us to keep trying and to stay focused on our goals. Resilience can't make problems disappear, but it can help us feel better and figure out what to do next.

At school, resilience helps us try new experiences and face challenges without feeling like giving up or thinking we can't do it. Instead of hiding or avoiding things that make us uncomfortable, we face them with courage and curiosity, wanting to learn and do well in school.

Resilience also helps us get along with our teachers and classmates. When someone says something we don't like or makes us feel sad or angry, we can take a deep breath and choose to make positive decisions to make things better.

Another important part of being strong is how we think. A growth mindset is one way of thinking that helps us make the most of what we can do and keep learning new things that can make us better. Having a growth mindset means that when things get tough, we are ready to try new ways of doing things, even if they are a bit scary. It's the belief that there's always a way to solve a problem, even if the first idea didn't work out.

Here are 30 resilience-building activities that can help you stay hopeful and keep trying until you reach your goals.

30 Weeks of Fun: Resilience-Building Activities for Fourth-Grade Students

The activities in this chapter are all about helping you become stronger and more resilient, while also teaching you how to think in a positive way. Over the next 30 weeks, you'll see how these activities can change the way you approach problems and deal with tough feelings. Get ready to be surprised by how much you can grow!

Activity 1: Recognizing Your Strengths and Challenges

Strengths are the things you are good at and challenges are the things you might need to practice more to get better at. When you know what you're good at and what you need to work on, you can figure out where you shine at school and where you might need more practice. That way, you can focus on improving the things you're not as strong in and celebrate even more strengths!

In the table below, write down some of your strengths and challenges at school. Examples of strengths could be:

- *doing math sums*
- *making friends*
- *listening in class*
- *On the other hand, your challenges could be:*
- *asking for help*
- *completing work on time*
- *writing neatly*

My strengths	My Challenges

Activity 2: Spotlight on Resilient World Leaders

Imagine stepping into the shoes of a legend like Mother Teresa, Mahatma Gandhi, Thomas Edison, Martin Luther King, Helen Keller, or Malala Yousafzai!

For this activity, you are required to prepare a speech on a remarkable figure from the past or present who has proven to tackle challenges with courage and resilience. Dig deep into their stories, both in their personal and professional lives, then share their inspiring tales with your fellow classmates! And don't forget to dress the part on speech day to bring history to life!

Activity 3: Learning From Mistakes

Mistakes aren't something to worry about. They are like little helpers that show us how to do things better. If we never made mistakes, we wouldn't know how to handle things the right way.

This activity is all about learning from those little slipups instead of feeling sad about them. You will get to fill out cards where you write down mistakes you've made before and the things you learned from them. For instance, if you used to forget your homework at home, you probably learned that it's important to pack your backpack the night before so you don't forget assignments anymore!

The mistake I made was...

What I learned was...

The mistake I made was...

What I learned was...

The mistake I made was...

What I learned was...

The mistake I made was...

What I learned was...

The mistake I made was...

What I learned was...

Activity 4: Blindfolded Obstacle Course

Let's head outdoors for an exciting obstacle course adventure!

Pair up with a classmate and take turns being blindfolded while the other person guides you. Your job is to listen carefully to your teammate's directions as you navigate the obstacle course. This game is all about learning to stay calm when things get tricky and working together to solve problems.

Once you have finished the course, switch roles and guide your classmate back to the starting point. It's a fun way to practice teamwork and communication skills!

Activity 5: Who Can You Turn to for Help?

Sometimes, we all need a little extra help to figure things out or get some good advice. The great thing is that there are lots of people in your life who are ready to help whenever you need it. These helpers could be your family members, friends, teachers, or caregivers.

In this game, you'll sort different cards into groups based on who could give the best help when solving different problems. You have four categories to choose from: family members, friends, teachers, and caregivers (e.g., nannies, babysitters, and tutors). When you are done, discuss your groups with the person sitting next to you.

Your older brother made a hurtful comment to you. Who can you turn to for help?

Your stomach is sore and you can't focus in class. Who can you turn to for help?

You forgot the teacher's instructions and need someone to remind you. Who can you turn to for help?

A kid in the playground pushed you off the swing. Who can you turn to for help?

You feel overwhelmed by the chores you have to do at home. Who can you turn to for help?

You have trouble paying attention while your teacher is giving instructions. Who can you turn to for help?

You feel left out because you were not invited to a classmate's party. Who can you turn to for help?

You are stuck on a math problem while doing your homework at home. Who can you turn to for help?

You had a bad dream last night that caused you to wake up feeling upset. Who can you turn to for help?

You feel nervous about an upcoming spelling test. Who can you turn to for help?

Activity 6: Resilience Mind Map

Resilience is all about learning coping skills. Before you dive into them with your teacher, see how much you already know. Get a piece of paper and draw a big circle in the middle. Write "Resilience" inside the circle. Now draw five arrows going out from the circle. For each arrow, write down what you think resilience means to you. Then, chat as a group about what you all came up with. Raise your hand when you are ready to share!

Activity 7: Classroom Superhero

The best way to understand resilience is to practice describing it in different ways and in different scenarios. Classroom Superhero is a writing challenge that seeks to help you understand different ways to practice resilience at school.

Your job is to write a short story about a student who faces some challenges but finds ways to overcome them by being brave and positive. Think about at least three problems your character solves with courage. The second part of the challenge is to take turns reading your superhero stories to the class. You can find a blank page at the end of the chapter to write down your ideas and start brainstorming your story!

Activity 8: Making Sense of Your Needs

Have you ever felt sad or upset but didn't know why? Sometimes, you feel this way because you forget to think about what you really need. It's important to understand your needs and share them with your teachers, friends, and family so that things can go well at school and home.

In this activity, you will be asked six questions to help you figure out what you need and how to tell others about it. First, think about a time when you felt unhappy, and then answer these questions:

1. What made you unhappy? Describe the situation.

_____

_____

_____

_____

_____

_____

_____

_____

_____

_____

_____

_____

_____

_____

2. What did you expect would happen? What were you hoping for?

_____

_____

_____

_____

_____

_____

_____

_____

_____

_____

_____

3. Did you express your wishes? Were other people aware of what you were hoping for?

_____

_____

_____

_____

_____

_____

_____

_____

4. How can you communicate your wishes in a positive manner? What can you say next time?

_____

_____

_____

_____

_____

_____

_____

_____

_____

_____

5. What positive steps can you take if the situation doesn't change after you have communicated your wishes? Who can you turn to for help?

_____

_____

_____

_____

_____

_____

_____

_____

_____

_____

Activity 9: Letter of Encouragement

When you're having a tough day, you need a little reminder that you are an amazing rockstar who can get through anything! Write a letter to yourself with kind and happy words that can cheer you up. Remind yourself of all the things that make you strong and awesome. Fold the letter and keep it in a folder so that you can read it whenever you need a boost of confidence. Use the blank page at the end of the chapter to write your special letter.

Activity 10: Visualizing Your Goals

Do you have any cool goals you want to achieve? I'm sure you do! A fun way to stay motivated is to look at pictures of your goals every day. In this activity, you'll make a vision board, which is a collage of photos that show what you want to achieve in different parts of your life, like school, friendships, and hobbies.

Bring some magazines from home and cut out pictures that capture your goals. For example, if you want to get better at a sport, find a picture of someone playing that sport, then cut it out and glue it on your board. By the end, you'll have a board full of goals and dreams that you hope to make a reality one day!

Activity 11: Calming Breath Meditation

Taking deep breaths helps you feel at ease. However, if you desire to feel even more relaxed, you can try meditating. Meditating means slowing down your busy thoughts so that you can feel calm. You can meditate anywhere, whether you're in your bedroom or at your school desk. Just five minutes of meditation can help your mind and body feel much lighter. In this activity, your teacher will guide you through a breath meditation, where you will focus on your breathing.

Script

Sit back in your chair and place your hands gently on your lap. Relax your shoulders and take a deep breath. Close your eyes and start paying attention to your breathing. Is it fast or slow? Does your breathing have a pattern?

Breathe in and out. Follow your belly as it rises and falls with each breath. Keep observing your breath as it flows through your body. How do you feel right now? Are you calm? Enjoy the deep relaxation that comes with each breath. On the count of three, slowly open your eyes. One, two, three.

Activity 12: Resilience Quotes

Sometimes, you might not know how to cheer yourself up during tough times. Luckily, millions of people have shared encouraging words online that can inspire you to keep going.

This fun activity needs a digital device so that you can search for five quotes about resilience. After finding your quotes, write a few sentences about what each one means to you. Here are some child-friendly websites to help you find your resilience quotes:

- *Mental Health Center Kids:* https://mentalhealthcenterkids.com/blogs/articles/growth-mindset-quotes
- *Better Kids:* https://betterkids.education/blog/13-resilience-quotes-for-kids
- *Such a Little While:* https://www.suchalittlewhile.com/growth-mindset-quotes-for-kids/

Activity 13: Problem-Solving Scavenger Hunt

Solving tricky problems means asking questions, thinking clearly, and being patient with yourself and others while you try out potential solutions. To practice these skills, get ready for a fun game of Problem-Solving Scavenger Hunt!

In this game, you and your small group will read clues to find items in different parts of the classroom (and maybe outside, too). When you find an item, put it in a box or bag. At the end of the scavenger hunt, you will reveal the items and see if you collected the right ones.

The goal of this game is to work together as a team to overcome challenges that might feel too big to handle alone. Here are the clues to start your scavenger hunt. Each group will start at different points so that you don't bump into each other.

Clue: *I help you write your name or draw a doodle. Look for me in the pencil holder.*

Clue: *I'm something you use every day; I'm full of sheets for work and play. Look in your desk or backpack to find me today.*

Clue: *I'm sticky and small; I help papers stick to the wall. Find me near the teacher's desk or a supply shelf.*

Clue: *I help you keep things together with a click. Look for me near the stapler or on the teacher's desk.*

Clue: *I have pages to turn, with stories to learn. I'm on a shelf, where knowledge is earned.*

Clue: *I provide shade on sunny days and a home for birds. Look high and low to find me.*

Clue: *I sparkle under the sun but turn dark when wet. Find me scattered on the ground where kids often play.*

Clue: *I'm green in the spring and summer but turn brown in the fall. I blanket the ground and make it soft.*

Activity 14: Pick-Me-Up Poetry

Poetry is a great way to share your thoughts and feelings on paper by using describing words, comparisons, and vivid pictures to show how you feel. Write your own resilience poem using a cinquain poem, which has five lines and is structured like this:

- *Line 1:* Write down one noun.
- *Line 2:* Write down two adjectives.
- *Line 3:* Write down three action words ending in "-ing."
- *Line 4:* Write a phrase made up of four words.
- *Line 5:* Write down a synonym for your topic.

Here is an example of a resilience poem created using the cinquain structure:

- *Resilience*
- *Brave, strong*
- *Breathing, focusing, problem-solving*
- *Keep taking small steps*
- *Courage*

Now it's your turn. Use the lines provided below to create your resilience poem. When you are done, take turns reading them out loud to the rest of the class.

Activity 15: Creating SMART Goals

Whenever you are motivated to learn a new skill or pick up a new hobby, establish meaningful goals to help you plan what steps to take. SMART goals have five cool elements that make them helpful in achieving what you want. They are specific, measurable, attainable, relevant, and time-bound.

In this activity, you will get to practice creating a SMART goal for something you want to do. Answer the questions to help you brainstorm the goals, then write a goal statement at the end.

1. What is your wish? Summarize your wish in a clear sentence.

_____

_____

_____

_____

_____

_____

_____

_____

_____

_____

_____

_____

_____

_____

_____

_____

_____

_____

2. Why is this wish important to you? How can it benefit your life?

_____

_____

_____

_____

_____

_____

_____

_____

3. How will you know when you have achieved your wish? Write down a few signs to look out for.

_____

_____

_____

_____

_____

_____

_____

_____

_____

4. What action steps can you take to get started? Write down five detailed steps.

_____

_____

_____

_____

_____

_____

_____

_____

_____

_____

5. When will you achieve the goal? Write down an end date.

_____

_____

_____

_____

_____

_____

_____

_____

_____

_____

_____

Activity 16: The Inner Critic, the Inner Cheerleader

Sometimes, you might find yourself in a tough situation that makes you feel scared or disappointed. Maybe, during recess, you made choices that got you sent to the principal's office, or maybe you didn't get the grade you were hoping for, and now, you're upset with yourself. During these moments, a small negative voice in your head, called the inner critic, might come out and say mean things like "How can you be so careless?" or "You are a bad friend."

The best way to counter this voice is to wake up your inner cheerleader, the small positive voice in your head that cheers you on. This voice reminds you of your strengths and encourages you to get back up and try again. For this activity, take the words spoken by the inner critic and turn them into words your inner cheerleader would say.

You are weird.

Why can't you be like other children?

Your ideas don't make sense.

No one likes you.

You never do anything right.

Everyone is smarter than you.

You are so lazy.

You should give up now.

Something is wrong with you.

You are too slow.

Activity 17: Classroom Strengths Assessment

It can be tough to know how you're doing in school when you're not sure what you're good at and what you might need a little help with. The "Classroom Strengths Assessment" is a checklist you can use each term to see how you're doing with different classroom tasks. Your job is to check whether each task is a strength or a struggle. After you finish the assessment, set up a time to talk with your teacher one-on-one about your progress.

Classroom Task	Strength?	Struggle?
Creativity: Using your own ideas to complete projects and assignments.		
Group work: Working well with classmates in group activities.		
Participation: Joining in class discussions and activities.		
Organization: Keeping your desk and materials neat and ready.		
Behavior: Following classroom rules and being respectful to others.		
Homework: Completing and turning in homework on time.		
Math Problems: Solving math problems correctly.		
Listening: Paying attention and following instructions.		

Writing: Writing clear and organized sentences and paragraphs.		
Reading Comprehension: Understanding and explaining what you read.		

Activity 18: Celebrate Your Small Wins

How often do you take a moment to give yourself a pat on the back and see how well you're doing? Staying focused and motivated during the year means regularly pausing to celebrate the small victories you achieve in the classroom, like learning new words, remembering to bring your homework, or finally feeling confident enough to raise your hand and join in class discussions.

Make it a habit to write down your small wins so you can keep track of your growth and learning. Turn to the end of the chapter to find the chart.

Activity 19: Ideal Life Portrait

Imagine your life as amazing as it can be–you're doing great at school, getting along with your siblings, having fun with your hobbies, and spending time with awesome friends. Draw a picture of what this perfect life looks like (use the blank page at the end of the chapter), then use the lines below to write down the steps you can take to make your vision come true.

_____

_____

_____

_____

_____

_____

Activity 20: ABCs of Gratitude

Think of one thing you are grateful for. Now think of two things you are grateful for. How about finding 26 everyday moments in life that you are grateful for? Could you do that?

The ABCs of Gratitude is a fun challenge that helps you find many reasons to smile and feel happy about your life. Your job is to go through the letters of the alphabet, from A to Z, and find something you appreciate that starts with each letter. Here is an example:

- *A for Access to education*
- *B for Brothers that I love*
- *C for Comfortable clothes*

Fill out the cards and cut them out when you are done. You can laminate them and punch a ring binder through them so they can last a long time.

| A |
| A for... |
| |

| B |
| B for... |
| |

C
C for...

D
D for...

E
E for...

F
F for...

G
G for...

H
H for...

I

I for...

J

J for...

K

K for...

L
L for...

M
M for...

N
N for...

O
O for...

P
P for...

Q
Q for...

R
R for...

S
S for...

T
T for...

U
U for...

V
V for...

W
W for...

X
X for...

Y
Y for...

Z
Z for...

Activity 21: Circle of Support

You don't need to face tough times alone when you have a support system of friends and family who can listen and help you solve problems. To see how big your support system is, draw a Circle of Support.

Start by drawing a big circle on paper. Inside that big circle, draw a smaller circle in the center. In the smaller circle, write the names of people you feel safe talking to about your feelings, like your parents, siblings, aunts, uncles, grandparents, and close friends. In the outer circle, write down the names of people who give great advice and help you succeed in school, social life, and sports. This might include your teachers, school counselor, sports coach, tutor, and doctor.

And there you have it! A group of people who are there for you when you need comfort and practical solutions to solve problems.

Activity 22: Affirmation Wall

Clear a spot on your classroom wall and turn it into an affirmation wall where anyone can post sticky notes with positive phrases and quotes to keep the class motivated. The wall can also be used for appreciation shoutouts to classmates who go above and beyond to help others and show kindness. Your challenge as a class is to fill up the affirmation wall with lots of colorful sticky notes filled with heartwarming messages that anyone can read during free time.

Activity 23: What Is Your Body Telling You?

Your body is always sending signals to your brain, letting it know how you're doing. For example, when you're cold, your body might shiver to tell your brain that it's time to wear a jacket or close the windows. Listening to your body helps you respond faster when you're tired, hungry, upset, or confused.

To practice this, close your eyes and take three deep breaths, then ask yourself, "How am I doing?" Listen for any signals from your body for clues. Here is a list of signals that might show up and what they mean:

- **Shivering:** Your body is cold and needs warmth, like putting on a jacket or closing the windows.
- **Stomach growling:** You're hungry and need to eat something.
- **Yawning:** You're tired and need rest or sleep.
- **Frowning or crying:** You're upset or sad and might need to talk to someone or take a break.
- **Tight jaw or shoulders:** You're feeling stressed or anxious and might need to relax or take deep breaths.
- **Sweating:** You're hot or nervous and might need to cool down or drink water.

- **Feeling fidgety:** You're restless and might need to move around or take a short walk.
- **Headache:** You might be dehydrated, tired, or stressed and might need to drink water, rest, or take a break.
- **Clenched fists:** You're angry or frustrated and might need to calm down or talk about your feelings.
- **Smiling:** You're happy or content and can enjoy the moment or share your joy with others.

Activity 24: Resilience Movie Marathon

This week, follow a movie character's journey to becoming more resilient. Watch at least one of the movies listed below (or both if you have enough time). You can watch them at school or as a homework task. While these movies are fun to watch, keep an eye on how the characters show resilience. After watching, you will talk about some questions in class to explore what you learned.

Movie: Akeelah and the Bee
Duration: 112 minutes
Age restriction: PG
Discussion questions:
- *What challenges does Akeelah face in her journey to the spelling bee? How does she overcome them?*
- *Who helps Akeelah build her resilience? How do they support her?*
- *What personal strengths does Akeelah use to succeed in the spelling bee? How can you relate these strengths to your own life?*

Movie: Brave
Duration: 93 minutes
Age restriction: PG
Discussion questions:
- *What challenges does Merida face in the movie? How does she work to overcome them?*
- *How does Merida's relationship with her family change throughout the movie? How does her family help her build resilience?*
- *What fears does Merida confront? How does facing these fears help her become more resilient?*

Activity 25: Creating Symbols

There are many fun ways to show what resilience means, and one of them is through symbols. Symbols are everyday objects that can have special meanings. They help us understand big ideas using pictures and comparisons.

Normal classroom objects can be turned into symbols that show resilience. For example, a pair of scissors can be a symbol of strength and focus because of the sharp blades. A notebook can be a symbol of perseverance because it has many pages to keep writing on.

For this activity, find an object in the classroom that symbolizes resilience to you and write a short paragraph explaining why.

Activity 26: Seeking Progress Over Perfection

No one in the world is a perfect student, but there are millions who try their best at school. Perfection might seem like a goal we can reach, but in reality, it doesn't exist, because mistakes do happen when we learn new things or take tests. Instead of feeling bad when we fail, we should focus on the progress we make.

This activity helps you focus on progress instead of perfection. Every small step in the right direction is progress because it helps you grow. In the table below, read the "perfect" statements and create "progress" statements that are more realistic. For example, instead of saying "I will get 100% on my math test," you could say "I hope to pass my math test" or "I hope to get more answers right on this test than I did on the last one." Remember, progress celebrates the little steps that help you move forward.

Perfect statements	Progress statements
I will never make a mistake when completing homework.	
I will get straight A's for every school subject.	
I need to make everyone happy all of the time.	
I will always be positive and never have a bad day.	
I will be the best player on my football team.	
I need to have perfect handwriting.	

Activity 27: Resilience Board

Help your teacher find a special spot in the classroom for a bulletin board that inspires and motivates everyone. Your teacher will regularly pin positive quotes, fun articles, announcements, and student achievements to spread good news and create a happy, thankful atmosphere. Check out the board once a week to see the latest exciting updates. If you have any good news to share, talk to your teacher about adding it to the bulletin board!

Activity 28: School Cleanup Project

It's up to you to help take care of your school so that it stays safe and welcoming for everyone.

Team up with your classmates in small groups and think of a small cleanup or maintenance project you can do in the classroom or around the school. You can start by walking around to spot any problems you could fix. For example, you might notice trash in the playground or messy shelves in the library.

After your walk, gather together and brainstorm ideas for solutions. Try out your idea to see if it works, then share it with the class. In the end, everyone will vote for one project to be done, and you will all work together to make it happen!

Activity 29: Prioritizing Tasks

Not every task that seems important is a good use of your time. When you have a lot of work piled up on your desk, you need to sort through tasks that are urgent and tasks that can be pushed to the side for now.

Prioritization means ordering your tasks from most to least important and working on the important ones first until you have finished all the tasks. To help you learn prioritization skills, you can use the Eisenhower Matrix, a tool that groups tasks into four categories:

1. Urgent and important (e.g., submitting an assignment due tomorrow morning)
2. Not urgent but still important (e.g., making study notes for an upcoming test)
3. Urgent but not important (e.g., watching the latest episode of your favorite TV show)
4. Not urgent and not important (e.g., scrolling through TikTok during free time)

Write down a list of your daily tasks on the lines below, and then assign each task to the appropriate block on the Eisenhower matrix. Submit the matrix to your teacher so that she can evaluate your work.

	Urgent	Not urgent
Important		
Not important		

Activity 30: Support Buddies

When you're not feeling your best, you can talk to a friend in your class who will listen and share kind words. A support buddy is a classmate chosen by your teacher to show kindness to you during tough times. In turn, you will be someone else's support buddy, caring for them when they face challenges. You don't have to solve their problems; just listen and encourage them with positive words. If you're worried about your classmates, it's important to tell them to talk to your teacher or another adult who can help them.

Developing resilience inside and outside of the classroom is crucial for your well-being. Whenever trouble comes, you will have a toolbox full of helpful coping strategies that can help you calm your mind, control your emotions, and make the best choices when it comes to your behavior.

Use the space below to write down your ideas and start brainstorming your short story based on the instructions given in Activity 7.

Use the space below to write your letter of encouragement based on the instructions given in Activity 9.

Use the chart below to record your small wins based on the instructions given in Activity 18.

Date	Small win	How do you feel?

Date	Small win	How do you feel?

Use the space below to draw a picture portraying your ideal life based on the instructions given in Activity 19.

Chapter - 6

Fifth Grade-Applying SEL in Daily Life

Keep your face to the sunshine and you cannot see a shadow.

- Helen Keller

Applying Social-Emotional Learning

Do you want to try a tongue twister? Practice saying "social-emotional learning" quickly 10 times without getting the words mixed up!

Social-emotional learning, or SEL for short, is all about helping you feel confident in sharing your thoughts, expressing your feelings in a good way, making smart choices, and working well with your classmates.

The main goal of SEL skills is to help you make a positive impact at school, at home, and in your community. That's right! These skills are useful in all parts of your life, helping you be ready for anything that comes your way.

SEL skills also help you deal with tough problems you can't avoid. For example, if you're nervous about an upcoming presentation, there are skills to help you calm your mind and manage your emotions. If you think that your parents have set unfair rules, some skills can help you talk to them without yelling or fighting. If you see a problem at your school or in your community, like littering or bullying, you can use SEL skills to work with others to find and solve the problem.

Below are 30 fun activities you can do over 30 school weeks. These activities will help you learn and practice SEL skills. Some activities can be done in the classroom, while others are meant to be done at home or in your community. As you go through these activities, remember the main purpose of learning SEL skills: to manage your thoughts and emotions responsibly, make positive decisions, and work well with others.

 30 Weeks of Fun: Activities to Help Fifth-Grade Students Apply SEL in Everyday Life Situations

Have you ever been in a new situation where you weren't sure what to do? As you grow up, you'll find yourself in lots of these tricky moments. When life surprises you, knowing how to handle it can make things much better. The activities in this chapter will help you feel ready to face any uncomfortable situation so that you can feel confident at school, at home, and in your community!

Activity 1: Role-Playing Scenarios

It's more fun to act out SEL skills than just talk about them. Wouldn't you agree? Your teacher will put you into groups and give you a theme to act out together. The theme will be about a special SEL skill like:

- *managing strong emotions*
- *resolving conflict*
- *asking for help*
- *standing up for yourself*
- *making the right choice in a bad situation*
- *listening to others without interrupting*

Get ready to prepare a short skit that shows the skill in action. Make sure everyone in your group has a part to play. After your skit, explain it to the class and share why you chose to show the skill that way. Have fun and be creative!

Activity 2: Problem-Solving Workshop

Solving problems can be fun and exciting! With the right tools, you can become a problem-solving hero.

Your teacher is planning a special problem-solving workshop in the classroom. To get ready, think of a real-life problem you have and write it down on a piece of paper. During the workshop, your teacher will show you different ways to solve problems. Use your problem to try out each method.

At the end of the workshop, share which method you liked the most and which one you liked the least, and state why.

Activity 3: Conflict Resolution Workshop

Put your textbooks away and get ready for a fun conflict resolution workshop! In this workshop, you'll learn cool ways to solve conflicts respectfully and positively. Your teacher has a special program for you, including discussions and activities on

- *defining conflict*
- *recognizing strong emotions*
- *using positive communication*
- *going through problem-solving steps*
- *presenting a conflict resolution model (like Stop, Talk, Listen, Think, Resolve)*

Your teacher will keep the workshop exciting with stories, videos, role-playing, and group projects, and give you a chance to share your thoughts and insights at the end. Get ready to learn how to handle conflicts like pros!

Activity 4: Success Iceberg

Icebergs are huge pieces of ice that float in the ocean. What's really cool is that we only see a tiny part of them, about 16 feet above the water, but they go as deep as 600 feet underwater!

Achieving success in school is a lot like an iceberg. People might see your good grades and awards, but they don't see all the hard work you do to get there. They don't see the hours you spend studying, the weekends you stay home to make notes, the times you ask your teacher for help, or the many books you read.

For this activity, think about the habits you need to reach a goal related to school or your hobbies. At the end of the chapter, you'll find a picture of an iceberg. Above the water, write down the achievements people see. Below the water, write down all the hard work and habits that help you reach your goal.

Activity 5: Famous Setbacks and Comebacks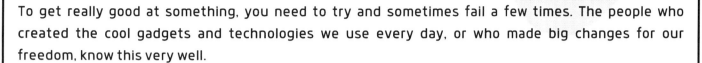

To get really good at something, you need to try and sometimes fail a few times. The people who created the cool gadgets and technologies we use every day, or who made big changes for our freedom, know this very well.

Your job is to pick a famous person who faced big failures before they solved a problem. Find out about their life, how they got started, the tough times they went through, and how they finally succeeded. Then, write a speech about this person and share it with your class.

Activity 6: Gratitude in Action

Often, when we think about gratitude, we think of saying "Thank you." But gratitude can also be shown through our actions. Gratitude in Action is an activity that helps you show appreciation to someone who has helped you learn, stay safe, or feel cared for at school, at home, or in your community. This could be your teacher, counselor, therapist, parents, classmates, or even pets.

Think about a small, kind act you can do to show how thankful you are for their support. Here are some fun ideas:

- *Buy a small gift.*
- *Cook their favorite meal.*
- *Do their chores.*
- *Write a special card.*
- *Go out for ice cream together.*
- *Spend the afternoon playing together.*

Activity 7: Family Trivia

How much do you know about your family? In this activity, you'll have fun chatting with different family members and learning more about their interests, hobbies, and preferences. Follow these simple steps to play:

1. *Talk to each family member and ask them questions.*
2. *Write down their answers.*
3. *If you can't talk to someone in person, you can call them or send a text to get their answers.*

Here are the questions to ask:

- *What is your favorite hobby?*
- *What is your favorite food?*

- *What is your favorite book or movie?*
- *What is your favorite color?*
- *What is one thing you love to do on the weekends?*

Bring the information to school and write an essay introducing each member of your family and the interesting facts you have learned about them. Have fun discovering more about your family!

Activity 8: Values Exploration

Values are the important things that guide your life. They shape how you think, solve problems, and stay motivated. When you're in a confusing situation, remembering your values can help you decide what to do.

This activity will help you find your core values related to school. These are the five key principles that help you do your best, solve problems, and stay motivated at school. Remember, your values might be different for other parts of your life, like with friends, family, or your health, and that's perfectly fine.

To start, think about everything that matters to you when it comes to learning, doing schoolwork, and getting along with your classmates. Circle the values from the table below that stand out to you.

Respect for others	Communication	Community	Punctuality
Teamwork	Support	Acceptance	Goal-setting
Determination	Independence	Accountability	Embracing change
Hardwork	Creativity	Doing your best	Compassion
Courage	Fun	Encouraging others	Listen to others

From the values you circled, pick your top five and write them down in order, starting with the most important one. Next to each value, write an example of what it looks like. For example, if you choose "Fun," you might enjoy doing group projects, joining in class discussions, or using technology to learn new things.

_____

_____

_____

_____

_____

_____

_____

_____

_____

_____

_____

_____

_____

_____

_____

_____

_____

Place your list of core values somewhere safe so that you can continuously remind yourself about what matters most to you at school, and make choices that match your values.

Activity 9: Making Your "Yet" Crown

There may be some school subjects or things you're still working on. This doesn't mean you won't get them; it just means you haven't mastered them yet. The word "yet" is powerful because it shows you're on your way to reaching your goals. It might not happen tomorrow or next week, but it will happen someday.

In this activity, you'll write down all the school goals you're still working on and put them on a paper crown that you can wear around the classroom or at home.

The materials that you will need for your crown include:

- *thick paper*
- *pencil*
- *ruler*
- *scissors*
- *staple gun*
- *marker*
- *coloring pencils*

Here are the instructions for making your "yet" crown:

1. *Take a piece of paper and hold it up and down.*
2. *Use a ruler to measure eight inches from the side, then draw a straight line. Grab your scissors and carefully cut along the line you just drew.*
3. *Next, turn the strip of paper sideways and measure five inches from the bottom., then draw a second line across the paper.*
4. *Starting from the left side, draw triangle shapes along the top line you just made. Make sure they're all the same size, and use a ruler if you want them to look extra neat.*
5. *Once you're happy with your spikes, carefully cut them out with your scissors. Erase any pencil marks left on your crown.*
6. *Write down your school goals on the crown. Afterward, get creative and use your favorite coloring pencils to decorate your crown!*
7. *Before you finish, check if your crown fits. Measure it around your head and if it's too small, don't worry! You can cut a smaller strip of paper (about two to three inches) and staple it inside your crown to make it fit perfectly.*
8. *Staple the two ends of your crown together, and place it on your head!*

Activity 10: Classroom Rules

Your classroom is whatever you make it! When you walk into the classroom with high energy and positivity, the atmosphere becomes vibrant and cheerful. But when you walk into the classroom with a frown on your face, everything starts to feel boring and irritating.

To create the classroom environment of your dreams, work together with your classmates to come up with some rules for your behaviors. Your teacher will allow each of you to present ideas, which she will write on the board in the form of a mind map. When you have enough ideas, you will go through a process of elimination to get down to 10 rules. Rules that receive the most votes get to stay on the board, and those that receive the least votes are erased.

At the end of each month, your teacher will reward one student in the class for showing a commitment to following the classroom rules. Each month will be a different student's turn to be recognized, so don't worry-you will get your turn!

Activity 11: Diversity Interview

You have a lot in common with your classmates, like being the same age, enjoying the same music, and watching the same TV shows. But some things make each of you unique, like having different family sizes or coming from different cultures. Find a classmate you don't usually talk to and pair up. Take turns asking each other the questions below to discover what makes each of you special.

QUESTIONS	ANSWERS
What language do you speak at home?	
Which country does your family come from?	
What are the staple foods eaten in your culture?	
What does your culture's traditional clothing look like?	
How many members do you have in your family?	
What are some family traditions that you enjoy?	

QUESTIONS	ANSWERS
What is something you have learned from your family that you will always remember?	
What special holidays does your family celebrate?	

Activity 12: Digital Scavenger Hunt

Browsing the internet is fun, however, the fun ends when you don't follow safety rules. Digital Scavenger Hunt is a group game that teaches you the best practices for keeping safe online, including the privacy and communication tips you need to know when surfing through apps and websites.

Get into groups of three or four and get access to at least one digital device like a computer, tablet, or laptop. Follow the scavenger hunt instructions to find all of the items listed. Note that this group project can also be done at home.

Instructions:

1. *Look for a website that teaches children about the importance of staying safe online. Write the name of the website on a piece of paper.*
2. *Find an article about cyberbullying and print it out. Take a highlighter and mark the key points mentioned.*
3. *Search for an app that helps children manage their screen time and provide a detailed explanation of how it works.*
4. *Research what the term "cookies" means and provide three solutions to protect yourself from internet cookies.*
5. *Find an article explaining what types of information you can share online and on platforms like social media, and what types of information must remain confidential. Print the article and highlight the key points with a marker.*

Activity 13: Self-Care Plan

Self-care means checking in with yourself regularly to see how you are feeling and what you can do to make yourself feel better. Self-care practices are healthy habits that help you respond to your needs. Below is a step-by-step guide to help you set up your custom self-care plan, which you can refer to whenever you are tired, lonely, bored, sad, or feel like having fun:

1. Mention five emotions that you experience often.

_____

_____

_____

_____

_____

_____

_____

_____

2. Set simple and actionable goals for each emotion. Your goals should focus on how you desire to manage your emotions. For example, when you are bored, your goal might be to find activities that can keep you busy.

_____

_____

_____

_____

_____

_____

_____

_____

3. Come up with a list of healthy activities that can help you achieve your goals. Aim for at least three activities per goal. You can include activities like reading, playing with your pet, squeezing a stress ball, talking to someone about your feelings, or drawing a picture.

_____

_____

_____

_____

_____

_____

_____

_____

_____

4. Decide on the best time to carry out your activities. For example, would it be better to carry them out in the mornings before school? During class? In the evenings? On the weekends?

_____

_____

_____

_____

_____

_____

_____

_____

5. Make a list of the people you can reach out to for help when you are struggling to cope with your emotions despite practicing these healthy activities. For example, if your self-care plan doesn't help you control anger, you can speak to your teacher, school counselor, or parents.

Activity 14: Collaboration Brainstorming

There is no such thing as a bad idea because ideas can be improved, especially when students work together to solve problems. As a class, you have been assigned a special case to help your teacher solve a classroom problem: Your classroom is often too noisy during group activities, making it hard for everyone to concentrate and learn.

Here is the information that your teacher has given you to help you think of solutions:

- *Currently, students talk over each other, making it hard for everyone to share their ideas and raising the noise levels in the classroom.*
- *During group projects, students often get up and move around, which adds to the noise.*
- *Your classroom isn't very large, so sound travels easily and quickly becomes distracting.*
- *Some students with louder voices dominate group discussions, making it difficult for quieter students to participate and be heard.*

Using the information given above, work together to solve the problem. Assign one person to write down all of the ideas and another person to be the referee, making sure everyone gets a turn to share their potential solutions. Finally, present the solutions to your teacher and go through the pros and cons of each, before choosing the best solution.

Activity 15: Quote for the Day

For the next month or so, each student in the class will get an opportunity to present the quote for the day. This should be a quote that is positive and inspirational. At the start of the day, before the lesson begins, the chosen student will stand up and share their quote, providing additional information like the author's name and what the quote means to them.

Here is a list of websites that you can use to find your quote and have it prepared for the day you present:

- *Emotionally Healthy Kids:* https://emotionallyhealthykids.com/100-best-inspirational-self-esteem-quotes-for-kids/
- *Good To Know:* https://www.goodto.com/family/children/inspirational-quotes-for-kids-539776
- *Little Yellow Star:* https://littleyellowstarteaches.com/2023/10/12/inspiring-quotes-for-kids/

Activity 16: Giving Back to Your School

You have a meeting with your school principal to talk about an important issue that needs everyone's help to solve. To fix the problem, your whole class will need to work together. You can choose to work in smaller groups of three or four, or you can all work together as one big group. Here are the steps you'll need to follow:

1. **Define the problem:** *Explain what the issue is.*
2. **Describe the impact:** *Talk about how the problem affects people.*
3. **Identify resources:** *Find out what tools or help you have to solve the problem.*
4. **Create an action plan:** *Make a step-by-step plan to fix the problem.*
5. **Set a time frame:** *Decide how long it will take to carry out the plan.*

Put all of these steps into one document and give it to your teacher. Your teacher will give you feedback and point out areas to improve. Once everything is polished, your teacher will give the documents to the principal, who will pick the best plan. Then, your whole class will work together to make that plan happen!

Activity 17: Emotions Expression Workshop

Most of the time, we use words to express our feelings. But did you know that creative arts like music, dance, acting, or drawing can also show how you feel?

This week, your teacher will hold an Emotions Expression Workshop. You can pick any art form to show an emotion of your choice! You'll get 10 minutes in class to plan, and the rest of the preparation will be done at home.

On the day of the workshop, you'll hand in your presentation to the teacher. If you're singing, dancing, or acting, you'll get to perform in front of the class. Lights, camera, action!

Activity 18: Mistake Analysis

Everyone makes mistakes, and it can feel frustrating when things don't go as planned. But mistakes are actually great opportunities to learn and grow! When you look at mistakes as lessons, you can figure out how to do better next time.

Here are some questions to ask yourself whenever you make a mistake at school or home. These questions are supposed to help you take a moment to pause and understand why you made a mistake and what you can improve next time. Remember, the goal is to learn and become better, not to feel bad about what happened.

Are you ready to explore and learn from your mistakes? Find a quiet spot and think carefully about the answers to these questions:

1. What happened? Describe the situation.

_____

_____

_____

_____

_____

_____

_____

_____

_____

_____

_____

2. What could you have done differently? What actions could you have taken to prevent the situation from happening?

_____

_____

_____

_____

_____

_____

_____

_____

_____

3. How can you make things better? What actions or choices can you make to fix the situation?

_____

_____

_____

_____

_____

_____

_____

_____

_____

4. What have you learned about yourself throughout this experience?

_____

_____

_____

_____

_____

_____

_____

_____

5. Who can help you to avoid making the same mistake again? What type of support do you need to learn new skills and behaviors?

_____

_____

_____

_____

_____

_____

_____

_____

_____

_____

_____

_____

_____

_____

_____

_____

_____

_____

_____

Activity 19: Classroom Behavior Checklist

Some behaviors help you focus and do your best in class, while others can be distracting and make it harder to pay attention and participate. This fun and simple checklist lets you think about your classroom behaviors to see what you're doing well and where you can get better. Check the box that best matches how you act in class. Remember, be honest!

QUESTIONS	ANSWERS	SOMETIMES	NEVER
I raise my hand when I have something to share with the class.			
I try my best to submit my homework on time.			
I keep my desk neat.			
I help my classmates when they need it.			
I greet my teacher and classmates every morning and say goodbye in the afternoons.			
I keep my hands to myself.			
I ask questions when I don't know what to do.			
I listen to the teacher when they are giving instructions.			
I work quietly during classwork time to avoid disturbing my classmates.			
I follow the classroom rules.			

Based on the checklist, what behaviors do you need to work on? Write them down below.

_____

_____

_____

_____

_____

_____

_____

_____

_____

_____

_____

_____

_____

_____

_____

_____

_____

_____

Activity 20: Conflict Resolution Practice

Conflicts with teachers or classmates can happen sometimes, and that's okay. Even if you mean well, your actions might sometimes upset others. Similarly, other people's actions can upset you and make you feel angry or sad. By practicing conflict resolution skills, you can learn how to handle these situations better.

Get into small groups and pick a scenario from the cards below to act out. Your skit should show both helpful and harmful ways of resolving the conflict. After your skit, explain it to the class so everyone can learn the best and worst ways to deal with conflicts.

Scenario 1	Scenario 2	Scenario 3
A student asks to copy another student's homework because they don't have time to do it.	Students in a group cannot agree on the best idea to use to complete a project.	A student borrows a ruler from another student and mistakenly breaks it.

Scenario 4	Scenario 5
A student keeps talking while the teacher is giving instructions, and eventually, the teacher gets annoyed.	A student starts a rumor about a classmate, which circulates the classroom and hurts the classmate's feelings.

Activity 21: Mindful Breaks

It's normal for your energy to go up and down during the school day. When you start feeling tired, it might be time for a mindful break!

Mindful breaks are short pauses between tasks. You can use them to stretch, go to the restroom, drink some water, or chat with a classmate. The idea is to step away from your desk and give your brain a rest so you can come back refreshed and ready to learn.

Work with your teacher to plan your mindful breaks. Decide together when you'll take them, how long they will last, and what you can do during the breaks. After a month, let your teacher know how helpful the breaks have been.

Activity 22: Active Listening Partners

Listening is something you can get better at with practice. For this activity, you'll team up with a partner to practice active listening. Stand facing your partner and take turns sharing how your day is going.

Here's the fun part: After each person speaks, the listener needs to repeat what they heard before sharing their own story. It might look like this:

- *Partner 1: My day started badly because I spilled milk on myself while eating cereal.*
- *Partner 2: So, you're saying that your day started badly because you spilled milk on yourself while eating cereal. Well, my day started on a happy note because I got to play my music playlist on the car ride to school.*
- *Partner 1: What I heard you say is...*

Practicing active listening requires patience, so have fun and take your time while completing this activity.

Activity 23: Affirmations Circle

Everybody has something special about them, including you. Form a circle with your classmates and sit down. Take turns going around the circle and mentioning something you love or find unique about yourself. Start your sentence with "I am..." For example, you might say "I am funny," or "I am passionate about cars." Listen carefully to every person's affirmation to learn more about what makes them special.

Activity 24: Family Engagement Activity

Did you know that spending time with your family can help you get better at social and emotional skills? This week, you have a fun challenge: Spend time with your family and then write a short essay about it to share with your teacher. Here's what to do:

1. *Gratitude Circle: Sit around the table with your family and take turns saying something you are thankful for.*
2. *Family Meeting: Have a family meeting to celebrate your achievements, talk about upcoming events, discuss any concerns, and reconnect with each other.*

In your essay, talk about how these two activities went. What did you learn about your family members? How did the activities make you feel? Which ones would you like to keep doing? Enjoy your time together and have fun writing about it!

Activity 25: Homework Helpers

Having support when completing homework can enhance your learning. For the next week, your teacher will assign you a homework helper. This is a classmate who you will work with to complete your homework assignments.

During the last 10 minutes of the day, you will be allowed to meet with your homework helper and get started with your homework tasks. If you are not able to complete the tasks within the allocated time, you can arrange to either meet after school or collaborate on a video conferencing platform like Zoom. At the end of the week, share feedback about how the experience went.

Activity 26: Letter to My Future Self

Fifth grade is your last year of elementary school before you head off to middle school. You might feel a mix of excitement and nerves about the changes ahead. To help you get ready for this big adventure, write a letter to your future self.

Share your thoughts and feelings about moving up to the next grade. What are you excited about? What makes you a little nervous? This is your chance to say whatever's been on your mind. Use the blank page at the end of the chapter to write your letter.

Activity 27: Careers Expo

What do you want to be when you grow up? Maybe you've thought about being a doctor, a teacher, an astronaut, or something else equally amazing! Maybe your desired career choice has changed several times since you were younger. Now, here's another opportunity to think about your dream job and learn more about it.

Get ready to share a speech about the job you want. Tell your classmates about it, like what you would do every day, what you need to learn to get the job, how much money you could make, and any cool perks that come with it. On the day of your speech, dress up like a professional in your chosen field to really get into character!

Activity 28: Weekly SEL Skills Checklist

To make sure that you are practicing your SEL skills regularly, here is a checklist that you can complete at the end of each week. Cut out the unmarked checklist below and make copies of it so that you can submit them to your teacher weekly. If you run out of checklists, you can ask your teacher to print more.

QUESTIONS	DIFFICULT	MODERATELY EASY	VERY EASY
Were you able to identify and express your feelings positively?			
Did you recognize what you were doing well and areas where you could improve?			
Did you practice seeing situations from different perspectives to understand where others are coming from?			
Were you able to show respect for other people's opinions, even when you disagreed?			
Did you listen to and cooperate with your classmates during group activities?			
Did you approach your teacher or classmate for help when you needed it?			
Were you able to brainstorm solutions for problems that you may have been facing?			
Were you helpful to classmates who needed support?			
Did you participate in classroom discussions and share your views?			

Activity 29: Peer Mentorship Program

To build friendships and practice social and emotional skills, you'll be paired with a student in a higher grade who will be your mentor. You'll only see them once in a while, so make the most of your time together! You can ask questions, talk about your favorite things, or get advice. Here are some fun ideas for your time with your mentor:

- *read a story*
- *play an educational game*
- *work on a homework assignment*
- *practice role-playing different social scenarios (e.g., problem-solving, conflict resolution, making friends, etc.)*

At the end of each mentoring session, reflect on what you have learned. To keep the conversation going while you are away from each other, you can exchange letters through your teacher.

Activity 30: Taking the High Road

Taking the high road means making good choices even when things are tough. Remember, you always get to decide how to react to situations. Think of a time when you made a good choice and it turned out well. Maybe you stood up for a friend who was being teased on the playground, or you told the truth about not finishing your homework, even though you might have gotten in trouble with your teacher. Write down your story and share it with the class. Let's learn from each other's good choices! Since SEL skills can be learned and practiced everywhere, and not just in class, why not challenge yourself to use these skills every day? You'll become a pro at understanding your feelings and making positive choices!

Around the iceberg below, write down the achievements that people see and the hard work it really takes to succeed based on the instructions given in Activity 4.

_____

_____

_____

_____

_____

_____

_____

_____

_____

_____

Use the space below to write a letter to your future self based on the instructions given in Activity 26.

Conclusion

Embracing Social-Emotional Learning

If not now, when? If not here, where? If not me, who?

- Steve Geiger

Social-emotional learning (SEL) is more than just a set of skills that students learn while at school. It is a fundamental developmental stage that empowers students to be the best version of themselves both inside and outside of the classroom. Equipped with these skills, students will display confidence in managing stressful situations, solving problems, communicating effectively with others, and modifying their behaviors according to each social context.

The purpose of this workbook is to introduce SEL skills at an elementary level to young students from kindergarten to fifth grade. Through age-appropriate interactive activities, students get the opportunity to engage with the skills and see firsthand how they can enrich their social and learning experiences.

If you have taken the time to present this workbook to your students and guide them through the activities, you have invested in their social, emotional, and behavioral growth. Your efforts could potentially change the trajectory of their academic careers and their interactions with people outside of the classroom, such as coaches, friends, family, and neighbors.

To continue the good work that you have begun, gain more knowledge and training on how to teach SEL skills and present them through fun activities. Transform your classroom into more than just a place of learning, but also a place of exploration and experimentation. Remember that the home counts as a place of learning too, so collaborate with parents to integrate these skills into students' daily lives.

Encourage your students to remain open to embracing challenges, cultivating positive relationships, and striving for personal and academic success with confidence and resilience. With the right attitude, there is no limit to the incredible milestones they can achieve!

If you have found this workbook effective for teaching and modeling good behaviors, please consider leaving a review on the Amazon page. Your thoughtful feedback can help other educators and parents locate this valuable resource!

Dear Reader,

Thank you for choosing to read my workbook. I sincerely hope it has provided you with valuable insights and practical guidance on your personal development journey. Your feedback is incredibly important to me.

If you found this book helpful or thought-provoking, I kindly request that you consider sharing your thoughts through a review. By doing so, you can help others discover the book and make an informed decision about whether it alights with their needs.

Leaving a review is quick and easy. You will just require your smartphone or tablet to scan the QR code below. This will take you to the review page for this workbook, and from there all you have to do is select a star rating, leave an honest review and click submit.

Your review will not only help me grow as an author but will also assist other individuals seeking guidance on their personal development journeys.

I appreciate your time and support. Thank you for being a part of this transformative experience.

Best regards,

Richard Bass.

About the Author

Richard Bass

Richard Bass is a well-established author with extensive knowledge and background on children's disabilities. Richard has also experienced first-hand many children and teens who deal with depression and anxiety. He enjoys researching techniques and ideas to better serve students, as well as providing guidance to parents on how to understand and lead their children to success.

Richard wants to share his experience, research, and practices through his writing, as it has proven successful to many parents and students.

Richard feels there is a need for parents and others around the child to fully understand the disability, or the mental health of the child. He hopes that with his writing people will be more understanding of children going through these issues.

Richard Bass has been in education for over a decade and holds a bachelor's and master's degree in education as well as several certifications including Special Education K-12, and Educational Administration.

Whenever Richard is not working, reading, or writing he likes to travel with his family to learn about different cultures as well as get ideas from all around about the upbringing of children especially those with disabilities. Richard also researches and learns about different educational systems around the world.

Richard participates in several online groups where parents, educators, doctors, and psychologist share their success with children with disabilities. Richard is in the process of growing a facebook group where further discussion about his books and techniques could take place. Apart from online groups, he has also attended trainings regarding the upbringing of students with disabilities and has also lead trainings in this area.

A Message from the Author

If you enjoyed the book and are interested on further updates or just a place to share your thoughts with other readers or myself, please join my Facebook group by scanning below!

If you would be interested on receiving a FREE Planner for kids PDF version, by signing up you will also receive exclusive notifications to when new content is released and will be able to receive it at a promotional price. Scan below to sign up!

Scan below to check out my content on You Tube and learn more about Neurodiversity!

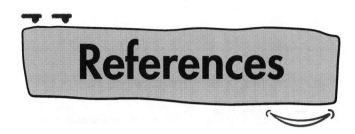

References

- *Am I in a healthy relationship?* (n.d.). Nemours TeensHealth. https://kidshealth.org/en/teens/healthy-relationship.html
- Arnwine, B. (2023, April 28). *What is a sensory toy and how can they help?* National Autism Resources. https://nationalautismresources.com/blog/what-is-a-sensory-toy-and-how-can-they-help/
- Autuori-Dedic, J. (2023, June 8). *4 big emotions to talk about with little kids.* Parents. https://www.parents.com/toddlers-preschoolers/development/intellectual/list-of-emotions-to-talk-about-with-kids/
- Beer, J. (2023, December 14). *How to apply social-emotional learning activities in education.* PositivePsychology.com. https://positivepsychology.com/social-emotional-learning-activities/
- *Blindfold game ideas.* (n.d.) Kid's Party Cabin. https://www.kids-partycabin.com/blindfold-game-ideas.html
- Bolt, U. (n.d.). *Usain Bolt quotes.* BrainyQuote. https://www.brainyquote.com/quotes/usain_bolt_447704
- Brubaker, A. (2022, October 6). *How to build people skills for students.* Connections Academy. https://www.connectionsacademy.com/support/resources/article/how-to-build-people-skills/
- CASEL. (n.d.). *Fundamentals of SEL.* Collaborative for Academic, Social, and Emotional Learning. https://casel.org/fundamentals-of-sel/
- Cherry, K. (2022, July 22). *5 reasons emotions are important.* Verywell Mind. https://www.verywellmind.com/the-purpose-of-emotions-2795181
- Chuter, C. (2020, January 13). *The importance of self-regulation for learning.* The Education Hub. https://theeducationhub.org.nz/self-regulation/
- Common Sense Media. (n.d.). *Twelve movies to help kids learn empathy.* Understood. https://www.understood.org/en/articles/12-movies-to-help-kids-learn-empathy
- Confucius. (n.d). *Confucius quotes.* BrainyQuote. https://www.brainyquote.com/quotes/confucius_101164
- Cronkleton, E. (2024, May 17). *Ten breathing exercises to try when you're feeling stressed.* Healthline. https://www.healthline.com/health/breathing-exercise
- Crowe, A. (2022, June 3). *17 fun team building activities for kids in your classroom.* Prodigy Game. https://www.prodigygame.com/main-en/blog/team-building-activities-for-kids/

- Dolan, K. (2023, May 3). How to make a crown out of paper (no glue needed!). Gathered. https://www.gathered.how/arts-crafts/how-to-make-a-crown-out-of-paper
- Early Childhood Mental Health Consultation. (n.d.). Ideas for teaching children about emotions. https://www.ecmhc.org/ideas/emotions.html
- Eng, J. (2023, July 10). Family-friendly songs to help kids deal with anger, sadness, and other big feelings. ParentsTogether. https://parents-together.org/family-friendly-songs-to-help-kids-deal-with-anger-sadness-and-other-big-feelings/
- Fowler, T. (n.d.). Feelings musical chairs. Teachers Pay Teachers. https://www.teacherspayteachers.com/Product/Feelings-Musical-Chairs-1135019
- Geiger, S. (n.d.). Steve Geiger quotes. Pinterest. https://in.pinterest.com/pin/786863366151110670/
- Greene, V. (n.d.). Vivian Greene quotes. Goodreads. https://www.goodreads.com/quotes/132836-life-isn-t-about-waiting-for-the-storm-to-pass-it-s-about
- Henley, W. E. (n.d.). William Earnest. Henley quotes. Goodreads. https://www.goodreads.com/quotes/7529528-i-am-the-master-of-my-fate-i-am-the
- Hsu, A. (2021, February 16). DIY clocks for kids: 9+ fun learning timepieces. Hello, Wonderful. https://www.hellowonderful.co/post/9-creative-diy-clocks-to-help-kids-tell-time/
- Hul, J. V. (2023, September 4). How to make paper plate masks for kids. The Artful Parent. https://artfulparent.com/how-to-make-paper-plate-masks/
- International Leadership Institute. (2019, January 30). Questions to ask when things go wrong. https://iliteam.org/coreleadership/questions
- Jess. (2021, June 29). The sensory benefits of rocking. Rhino Sensory UK. https://www.rhinouk.com/the-sensory-benefits-of-rocking/
- Johnson, S. (n.d). Samuel Johnson quotes. BrainyQuote. https://www.brainyquote.com/quotes/samuel_johnson_121919
- Keller, H. (n.d). Helen Keller quotes. BrainyQuote. https://www.brainyquote.com/quotes/helen_keller_120988
- Kris. (2021, December 6). 50+ ways to build relationships with kids and teens. The Pathway 2 Success. https://www.thepathway2success.com/50-ways-to-build-relationships-with-kids-teens/
- Kris. (2023, November 14). 25 self-control activities for children. The Pathway 2 Success. https://www.thepathway2success.com/25-self-control-activities-for-children/
- *Kris. (2024, June 18). 20+ strategies for teaching empathy. The Pathway 2 Success. https://www.thepathway2success.com/20-strategies-for-teaching-empathy/*
- *Louick, R. (2017, July 2). How to teach growth mindset to kids (The 4-week guide). Big Life Journal. https://biglifejournal.com/blogs/blog/teach-growth-mindset-kids-activities*
- *McCready, A. (n.d.). How to teach kids to say sorry: 3 steps for success. Positive Parenting Solutions. https://www.positiveparentingsolutions.com/parenting/how-to-teach-kids-to-say-sorry*
- *Mirgai, S. (2016, September 1). A body scan script. VHA Office of Patient Centered Care & Cultural Transformation. https://www.va.gov/WHOLEHEALTHLIBRARY/docs/Script-Body-Scan.pdf*

- Narvaes, A. (2022, February 22). Why stretching is important for your child and how you can make it fun. Mountain Kids Louisville. https://mountainkidslouisville.com/blog/stretching-important-child-can-make-fun/
- National University. (n.d.). What is social emotional learning (SEL): Why it matters for educators. National University. https://www.nu.edu/blog/social-emotional-learning-sel-why-it-matters-for-educators/
- Pathway 2 Success. (n.d.-a). Empathy board game for social emotional learning skills and perspective-taking. Teachers Pay Teachers. https://www.teacherspayteachers.com/Product/Empathy-Board-Game-for-Social-Emotional-Learning-Skills-Perspective-Taking-3688927
- Pathway 2 Success. (n.d.-b). Mindfulness game - SEL board game activity. Teachers Pay Teachers. https://www.teacherspayteachers.com/Product/Mindfulness-Game-SEL-Board-Game-Activity-4765486
- Pathway 2 Success. (n.d.-c). Self control game - SEL activity for self-regulation skills. Teachers Pay Teachers. https://www.teacherspayteachers.com/Product/Self-Control-Game-SEL-Activity-for-Self-Regulation-Skills-4556149
- Robinson, M. (n.d). Maria Robinson quotes. Goodreads. https://www.goodreads.com/quotes/186119-nobody-can-go-back-and-start-a-new-beginning-but
- Rushton, J. (2020, August 13). Building resilience in the classroom. CPD Online College. https://cpdonline.co.uk/knowledge-base/safeguarding/building-resilience-in-the-classroom/
- School of Education Online American University. (2021, June 15). How to incorporate mindfulness in the classroom. https://soeonline.american.edu/blog/mindfulness-in-the-classroom/
- Selby. (n.d.-a). Building strong connections: Teaching interpersonal communication skills in elementary school. Everyday Speech. https://everydayspeech.com/sel-implementation/building-strong-connections-teaching-interpersonal-communication-skills-in-elementary-school/
- Selby. (n.d.-b). How to teach perspective taking skills in elementary school: A practical approach. Everyday Speech. https://everydayspeech.com/sel-implementation/how-to-teach-perspective-taking-skills-in-elementary-school-a-practical-approach/
- Selby. (n.d.-c). Teaching elementary students how to ask for help: A guide for educators. Everyday Speech. https://everydayspeech.com/blog-posts/no-prep-social-skills-sel-activity/teaching-elementary-students-how-to-ask-for-help-a-guide-for-educators/
- Spickard, J. (2019, August 15). How music helps children connect with nature. Musikgarten. https://teacherblog.musikgarten.org/how-music-helps-children-connect-with-nature/
- Strong4Life. (n.d.). Get the conversation started with kids and teens. Strong4Life. https://www.strong4life.com/en/parenting/communication/conversation-starters-for-kids-and-teens
- Sullivan, J. (2019, July 18). Teaching students how to ask for help. Edutopia. https://www.edutopia.org/article/teaching-students-how-ask-help/

- Sutton, A. (n.d.). Types of poems for kids to read and write. Vibrant Teaching. https://vibrantteaching.com/types-of-poems-for-kids/
- Team Asana. (2024, January 29). The Eisenhower Matrix: How to prioritize your to-do list. Asana. https://asana.com/resources/eisenhower-matrix
- 10 activities for teaching young children about emotions. (2021, January 26). Paul H. Brookes Publishing. https://blog.brookespublishing.com/10-activities-for-teaching-young-children-about-emotions/
- Tiny bead confetti bracelet. (n.d.). KiwiCo. https://www.kiwico.com/diy/art-creativity/jewelry-fashion-design/tiny-bead-confetti-bracelet
- Vallejo, M. (2023, March 22). 20 growth mindset activities for kids. Mental Health Center Kids. https://mentalhealthcenterkids.com/blogs/articles/growth-mindset-activities-for-kids
- Warren, J. (n.d.). Feelings songs. Preschool Express. http://www.preschoolexpress.com/music-station09/feelings-songs-april.shtml
- Waterford. (2022, July 26). 52 journal prompts for kids to reflect and practice writing skills. https://www.waterford.org/resources/journal-prompts-for-kids/
- What is empathy? (n.d.). Center for Responsive Schools. https://www.crslearn.org/publication/the-power-of-empathy/what-is-empathy/
- What is resilience? (n.d.). ReachOut. https://schools.au.reachout.com/articles/what-is-resilience
- Williams, K. E., & Howard, S. J. (2021, February). Children's self-regulation: Why is it important and how can we support it? Emerging Minds. https://emergingminds.com.au/resources/childrens-self-regulation-why-is-it-important-and-how-can-we-support-it/
- Wilson, D., & Conyers, M. (2017, January 4). Four proven strategies for teaching empathy. Edutopia. https://www.edutopia.org/article/4-proven-strategies-teaching-empathy-donna-wilson-marcus-conyers/

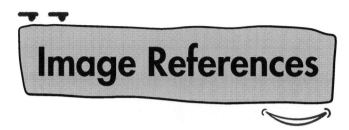

Image References

- ArtRose. (2021, November 4). Snowman christmas coloring book [Image]. Pixabay. https://pixabay.com/vectors/snowman-christmas-coloring-book-6763905/
- Artsy Bee Kids. (2020, October 23). Ladybug insect book [Image]. Pixabay. https://pixabay.com/illustrations/ladybug-insect-book-read-glasses-5676628/
- Bucarama-TLM. (2024, March 15). Flag nation drawing [Image]. Pixabay. https://pixabay.com/illustrations/flag-nation-drawing-cutout-8632191/
- Danilyuk, P. (2021, June 21). Boy in orange shirt playing on the floor [Image]. Pexels. https://www.pexels.com/photo/boy-in-orange-shirt-playing-on-the-floor-8422207/
- Fischer, M. (2020, August 28). Boy in brown jacket [Image]. Pexels. https://www.pexels.com/photo/boy-in-brown-jacket-5212315/
- Holmes, K. (2020, November 17). Positive black boy doing homework in copybook [Image]. Pexels. https://www.pexels.com/photo/positive-black-boy-doing-homework-in-copybook-5905479/
- Lach, R. (2021, June 29). Children peeking on a circular window [Image]. Pexels. https://www.pexels.com/photo/children-peeking-on-a-circular-window-8544502/
- Loring, V. (2021, May 12). Young students doing robotics together [Image]. Pexels. https://www.pexels.com/photo/young-students-doing-robotics-together-7869041/
- Madartzgraphics. (2017, February 16). Iceberg iceburg ice [Image]. Pixabay. https://pixabay.com/vectors/iceberg-iceburg-ice-glacier-frozen-2070977/
- Nilov, M. (2021, July 26). Kids writing on a whiteboard [Image]. Pexels. https://www.pexels.com/photo/kids-writing-on-a-whiteboard-8923027/
- Pixabay. (2019, September 3). School enrollment, school cone [Image]. Pixabay. https://pixabay.com/photos/school-enrollment-school-cone-4447737/
- Shuraeva, A. (2021, June 24). Girl in yellow sweater watching a boy playing with paper plane [Image]. Pexels. https://www.pexels.com/photo/girl-in-yellow-sweater-watching-a-boy-playing-with-paper-plane-8467296/
- Thirdman. (2021, July 27). Students raising their hands inside the classroom [Image]. Pexels. https://www.pexels.com/photo/students-raising-their-hands-inside-the-classroom-8926542/
- Tizas. (2019, April 24). Mandala beautiful flowers pattern [Image]. Pixabay. https://pixabay.com/vectors/mandala-pattern-flower-black-white-4151794/

Made in United States
Troutdale, OR
12/06/2024